At An Early Age

By

Red Jordan Arobateau

At An Early Age

Originally published 1977
Reprinted 2012

ISBN: 978-1-300-50379-8

Published by RED JORDAN PRESS
Redjordanarobateau.com
USA

INTRODUCTION

This flashy, short, fast moving black-centric novella EARLY AGE races along off the page, fresh from the ghetto into the reader's brain. It is historical fiction of those old black gay clubs & house parties.

Did not want this fine story to get lost, buried inside the anthology STORIES FROM THE DANCE OF LIFE, so decided to reissue it in it's own cover.

EARLY AGE has quite a bit of sexual content.

It's hero is hi-yella butch, Prince. A handsome Casanova. "Prince had the savoir-faire. Prince really knew how to love. Loving is more then just tenderness in bed, for a lot of women it is treating them like a lady out of it. Wining & dining them, buying them presents. Going out on a limb for her. Being good to her. In the clubs & restaurants she treated Selima like a lady. In bed she loved her allnight long."

The second main player, Flip, is a character who appears in several of Master Author Arobateau's novels -- BARS ACROSS HEAVEN, and HO STROLL.

"Prince always said she wanted to be a pimp; "Just to try it out and see what it bes like." And by now she had the qualifications. Plenty of women, charm that wouldn't wear out. She could get any lady she wanted. Black ones, white ones, Mexican ones, Orientals, Filipino's; gay ones, straight ones, and both-way ones; they all liked her."

In this tale we frequent some of the same lowlife dives we've been to before in Red's aforementioned works. We are introduced to a secession of ladies; women, fems; including fabulous Jet Black Della, Copper Colored Sadie, Sweet 'n Brown, voluptuous, Velda, hot hot mixed-race Japanese Shu-Shen.

There are poignant observations of Prince: "Prince had won the battle if anyone had. But, like acid, these things ate away at her. --Her lack of a job; abusive people-- both in varieties of black & white, and males and other women as well. And, worse, there seemed to be no union among women to soften the blows, or, to combat the hate.

'Women have to start getting together and doing something for ourselves.'

"Prince was treated by all who saw her as an idol. That was dangerous. "Everybody likes me yeah, but it's no good." Prince said this herself."

You won't want to deny yourself the treat of reading AT AN EARLY AGE, and it's startling, unexpected revelation that you will never forget!

At An Early Age

"Sure is a lot of fine women
in here tonight..... They are
women aren't they ?"

-- Yolanda (Prince) Henry; from
a conversation in the gay club
SOULVILLE.

Chapter One

"WHISKEY! WHISKEY!" Prince cried, draped over a chair.
"I'M DYING! HELP SOMEBODY HELP!" She needed a good stiff
drink. Leaned her curly head back over one arm of the chair, eyes
shut; "Della's after me calling over to Mommy's house, leaving notes
for me at work, and Xenia won't act right. OHHMAGAWD
GIRRRRL, what am I gonna do ?" And proceeded to kick her booted
feet over the other arm of the chair.

"Well...." Said Flip, the practical one, attempting to give
advice, "Decide which lady you like better, then, go after her."

"I don't have to go after either one, they're after ME! That's
the problem right NOW!"

Prince was a handsome gay blade, age 18. Slim, lean thighs,
flat chested--naturally--without binding; she sprawled out in the chair,
phone receiver to her ear. Her satin suit, wrinkled from last night
stretched across her shoulders. Her hair was curly, but not kanky.
She didn't have an ounce of extra fat on her. "Choose." Said the
voice over the phone.

"But.." She lamented, her features reflecting no emotion; ".. I
want 'em both."

Prince's father was a Director of a Mortuary -- epitome of black culture-- A Funeral Parlor mortician. They were middle class. The young woman had been raised with some money. She was a stone butch. Prince was Anglo in appearance. So light she could pass for white, that is she was taken for white easily. Her skin was absolutely white. Alabaster white. Couldn't get a tan. Only turned red--and her hair was wavy, which she styled for the maximum effect. Lips & nose were not exactly keen but not that Negroid. It was only when she opened her mouth you could tell-- and by her walk and her style.

And that was the key. Prince had style.

"So, what's been happenen'?" Came the voice thru the telephone line.

"Just everything. Men messing wit' me, no money, people at work; women won't act right..."

"Aw, I hear yuh. Same old thang huh..... How did it go last night with Della?"

"OK. But girrrll I ran into Xenia that woman I tole you about? She gave me her number girl. I walked by her in the club, she pressed it into my hand--written on a bar napkin."

"What's she look like?"

"Looks allright."

Prince spoke in her low, hard voice. In her head, sogged by alcohol from last nights partying down at the club SOULVILLE, a parade of events still lingered with its bells, painted women and perfume.

Della, her woman since the age of 16, and she, had been broken up for 6 months, but they still dated. That evening they'd gone to dinner, then Prince had taken her to the club.

6

It was that hardness, and the candy sweet image that women loved. Much flair. Black dialect, with which she rapped much shit into her ladies ear. Dressed like a pimp going mackin' for a down payment on a Cadillac---radiating a world of confidence. Candy.-- Ladies ate her up. That's something.-- When people eat up an image. Prince was well aware of her image, even at such an early age.

They'd strutted into the black discotheque. Prince had on a striped suit, vest, jacket, white shoes, ruffled shirt and a bowtie. Hair was to her shoulders, dark brown, wavy in a masculine cut-- notorious in the black male world --the Lord Jesus. Cute, but strong.

She escorted her lady to the bar. Many eyes in female heads turned to eye them jealously, but surface appearances can mislead. The relationship was not going well.

Now in a club gay folks see two women together they ASSUME, but it's not always the case. Prince & Della were by this point only friends, & as they bent over their glasses, slurping up a pink liquid liquor out of red straws, they were already having an argument in those low 'romantic' tones.

Della wore a plaid suit, skirt to her knees, jacket and women's vest. Was an attractive black complected woman, full lips, round eyes with long lashes. A bit of makeup tastefully applied. Lips with the wet look. Had her own hair, which was long, pressed, and worn up in a bun. Della was full breasted, full hips & she could shake-a-leg on the dance floor. An hourglass figure.

Gay folks at SOULVILLE was partying. Whistles blew. Tambourines banged. Voices shouted, others sang. Strong muscled legs danced to the rhythm. Ebony faces with Afros strained as they executed steps. Tall women like willows, Watusi's; some in men's suits, others in dresses. Slim as spiders. Short women like Pigmies bobbed, planting their feet then lifting them up in time to the rhythm. "YEAH WAHH!" Music with bells; when it started you couldn't resist it. Shoulder shaking, hip switching, posing, double beat, jumping, crouching. Hand motions. Some dancers stood on the sidelines, wiped perspiration off their faces and sipped drinks. Men danced with men, women danced with women, but all together in a wild mad crowd.

During the course of the night Xenia appeared on the scene. It was 1am--she'd just got off work, the night shift at a company downtown where she was a manager. Xenia was slim, an older woman of 34. 5'7", she was taller then Prince. Wilted from her 8 hours on the job but still attractive in a ladies pants suit with a string of beads. Prince looked down the bar & saw Xenia & continued rapping to Della without missing a syllable. Xenia kept her eyes glued to that white face down the bar amid the sea of black brown, and, before closing time had managed to slip her a wad of paper.

"WAL!" Crowd was moving to a tune. Double beat. "AH NEVAH BEN' IN SO MUCH LOOOOOOVE!" Figures ducking and weavin'. "NOW AH ' KNOWAH ALL 'DIS MUS' SOUND STRANGE. AH' SWEAH PLUEAAASE BAHBEE BAHBEEE!" Prince & Della stood together, their heads interlocking hairs they were so close. Lonely butches wandering past looked longingly at the attractive Della-- her dark brown legs in the skirt, she was a real lady, but, obviously taken. Only the bartender, or those right next to them might be able to make out the actual conversation however, as it went, above the rising din of the club-- as closing time approached. "Yo' fonky attitude, THAT'S what I'm talkin' about." Prince spoke, harshly.

"Well Prince! I didn't tell you you had to move out! That was your idea!" Cried Della in impeccable English.

Bells and drums ushered the vision along triumphantly. If only the two women could get it together and have some fun! But the rift between them was too large.

The bar was up front, about quarter of a block long, a hundred people stood there, or sat on barstools. Across a stretch of red carpet, and down two steps was the dance floor. Energetic dancers exhaled frustrations of their black & Colored lives breathing it out thru every pore, sweating as they jumped. Della & Prince danced athletically, both women's faces remained shut, tense. However, a slow record came on & their bodies came together. Prince coolly took the lead,

8

guiding her lady in a small circle. The heart beat of drums marched towards an orgasm. Maybe the two began to fall in love with love--- or the memories of how it had been those early months of their relationship when Prince was 16, and Della 18.

They went home. Della's tiny one room apartment in San Francisco's gay area. The dark woman bustled around hanging up their jackets in the closet, picking up some plates & put them in the sink. Prince went in the bathroom, dropped her pin stripped pants and sat on the toilet pissing out a stream of yellow urine that was acid from the drinks. Meanwhile she transferred the wad of paper into her wallet. It said:

XENIA, 423-5901. Call anytime. XXXXXX XXXXX

Prince strode out of the bathroom. Now she wore only her trousers & vest and ruffled shirt. Shoes kicked off. Della had turned back the covers. Shapely in her skirt & blouse--and, shorter. In her stocking feet. "Baby, it's good to have you here, and I had a wonderful evening."

"So did I."

The lights were dim, and Della was coming out of her blouse. Prince unbuckled her trousers.

Just friends, but friends do get down once & awhile.

Prince was not all glamour and show. In the bed she delivered. Della's flesh was velvet, soft. Clad in only her slip now, and wiggled out of her underpants. She reached for the light switch having a last glimpse of her butch, Prince, who stood, feet apart, coming out of her shirt, clad in a silk men's undershirt, her white arms glistening under the lights. CLICK. Now neon from the street illuminated the room. Prince came to the bed, Della lay on the sheet, the covers thrown back. Prince slid her hand down the woman's rounded buttocks and bent her curly head down to that face on the pillow which eagerly waited for her. "Do you want me Prince, do you? Just answer!"

9

"Don't you hear me talkin' baby?" Prince muttered as she ran her hands down Della's shoulders, then, pressed her thigh between Della's thigh, hard, until they parted, opening and hot. The two women had done that con job on each other-- the 'forever and ever'-- it hadn't worked out that way. But now they had something more precious between them-- old times. Memories. The thrill remembered, and experienced many times before.

"Ooohhh." Della sighed, she pulled away from her lovers arms and came out of her slip. Scent of underarms, and women's smell, mixed with perfume and Afro-Sheen hair relaxer. It was home. Prince grabbed Della again, burying her nose in the side of the woman's neck and nestles there a moment. Dark hands ran over her back, trying to peel off the teeshirt, and Prince was still in her trousers. "OH, come on baby, I'm ready!" The woman cried.

Prince stood up by the side of the bed, stripped quickly; flat white stomach, a mist of pubic hair, the rings on her fingers were the only thing she had on. The two nude women pressed together. Lips parted, slid into place, lips sucking on each others gently, then their tongues probing into each others mouths. Black hands caressing the strong back harder, as Prince gently pushed her down on the bed, and rolled on top. Della lay back as Prince lowered her curly head and began sucking the nipples of Della's full breasts. Squeezing the dark flesh with her white hands, running her tongue over each nipple 'till they were hard, then sucking them gently like a baby, while squeezing the breasts full round melons. With one hand she stroked the inside of the woman's hot thighs, which in response spread wider to accommodate her lover.

Prince did cuninlingus on her woman, running her tongue over and over her hard pearl clit while embracing her body lovingly, 'till the woman's hips thrust upward, nearing orgasm; then she rolled over, procured a device from the bedstand drawer, strapped around her thighs a phallus of soft skinned but rigid, hard rubber, lubricated this with jell and again in all seriousness mounted the waiting woman. Placed the tip of the phallus at the entrance to her vagina and slowly pushed in. In and out. Rapidly, she thrust. As she worked towards her own climax she satisfied Della also who was on the verge of orgasm. As Prince pumped and humped thrusting her organ rapidly

10

in and out of the woman underneath her, working the slow steady hot fire of pleasure towards satisfaction; in the back of her mind was the idea of meeting Xenia the next day. The affair with Della was over, they both knew it. In a moment a flood of release, then the two slept.

Chapter Two

The two butches continued their conversation via the phone. About 10 minutes had passed. Prince swallowed a drink of ice water. "I'm tired of her. She blew it last year when she started running around with dudes. Now she wants me back, but it's too late. She wore me out last night. And she don't do nuthin' for you, lay up there in the bed, gets to screamin' & hollerin' and clawin' my back. Woke me up all last night. Twice. To fuck.

This morning was allright. She was late to work. I gave her a facial massage. She went down on me girl for a half an hour, but I didn't get a nut. I topped her, everything, but, no dice. The thrill is gone.

She's got a nice rear end tho. You know I'm a Bootie Bandit."

"Yeah, I know. What is that again?"

"A Bootie Bandit is somebody who likes rear ends."

"I guess you gonna have to figure out whose got the best rear end. Della or the other one, what's her name...."

"I'm taken' the bull by the horns. Della is gonna have to do right, or she can't have me. And she can't do right so I'm goin' after Xenia."

"What are you gonna do about Della?"

"Later for that bitch." Growled Prince.

"I heard that!"

Chapter Three

Princes current job was a cook at the Hamburger Palace. $2.50 per hour--minimum wage. For all her style, good looks and intelligence it was a lowly job. The handsome butch never had enough cash ducats in her pockets.

The Hamburger Palace was tile and plastic. Brightly lit with florescent lights. The night howled outside full of blazing white headlights on cars coming, and red taillights going. Prince worked with a partner inside a glass cage, flipping burgers, while the sweat rolled down their faces. The customers stood outside waiting for their orders.

That evening an incident occurred. A nigger strode up to the counter--in his thirties, an ugly face, and a sullen disposition. He yelled at Prince thru the glass, "BITCH, MAKE ME A HAMBURGER."

Prince stared thru the glass at him, the white cooks cap on her curly head. "MY NAME AIN'T BITCH."

The nigger might have been drunk but that's only an excuse and it's no good. He acted that way when sober also. "BITCH! DON'T YOU KNOW I'LL SHOOT YO'!" He yelled, pressing his ugly face up to the glass.

Prince put her hands firmly on the counter, her mind charged with fear pictures. The emotions of a Chimpanzee in the jungle, terrified, of a bullet shattering the glass cage, aimed straight at her; but she allowed only the purest confidence to radiate out of her face, and yelled right back at the nigger; " SHOOT ME THEN GODDAMN IT! GO 'HEAD!" The man's face twisted with rage. He was use to taking to women this way & them accepting it docile, like cows, heads bowed.

"I'M HONGRY! MAKE ME A HAMBURGER! YO' AIN'T TALKEN' THAT SHIT WHEN I'M HONGRY!" Countered the ignorant nigger in disbelief.

"WELL I'M TIRED OF WORKING!" She yelled back & refused to serve him. Folded her arms, cooks cap fluttering on her head.

He staggered out, mumbling to himself; "'Ah don't believe the bitch tole me that."

Prince placed her hands on her hips and surveyed the dismal little crowd around her glass cage waiting patiently for their food; she said; "NOW! DO ANYBODY ELSE IN HERE WANT TO SHOOT ME?"

She worked hard, and got tired, & seemed to be getting nowhere.

Chapter Four

"HEY CHUMP!"

Prince cried-- her standard greeting upon seeing her buddy Flip, a little yellow nigger who dressed more masculine even then her. It was that attitude of disdain about Prince. The senior Flip found it disconcerting to be called 'Chump' but Prince got away with it. Like the member of a royal court who could address their subjects in any way they choose-- for her company was special. The two had met at a corner down in the Tenderloin--a hustling section of town not far from SOULVILLE. It was evening; red & green lights of taverns were on. They greeted and began to talk about the latest in their love lives, as they strode along the street.

Tonight, Prince's hair had gone bush. She'd wrapped it in curls to make it kinkier, let the curls set, then blown it out into an Afro. Curls For the Girls. Her face was solemn, and as they passed under a tavern marquee, green lights flooded it for a moment. "You know, they ought to have a city with only women. Just women. No

13

men allowed.-- Just to pass thru. No. Not even that. Make the FLY over."

Prince was young, but for that old voice of hers, that young-old voice. There were too many hostile influences in the world she was beginning to see thru her teenage eyes.

Flip was older, at 28 she'd seen life in a half dozen American cities. "I 'kin dig it." She responded.

The two women stepped up to Flips car and climbed inside. Flick of the knob and music filed the interior. They kicked back in comfort of modern seats. The radio station played the latest hit. Hot grinding thigh-locked-in-thigh type of songs.--Two women loving each other, pressing cock to cock. "These songs incite you to riot." Flip muttered.

"You ain't never lied." Replied Prince gruffly.

They drove slowly thru the crowded downtown section, Flip maneuvering the wheel, eyes keen under her blue hat brim. "You look good." She said giving Prince a casual look. "Folks probably think you're a goddamn pimp." She added.

"I ain't never seen a pimp that looks this good." Said Prince.

"Huh huh." Flip chortled coming to stop at a red light. Looked over at her buddy who gesticulated:

"No kidding! Wearin' suits with the linings out and shit!" & turned the lapel of her suit inside out to demonstrate.

The car slowly gained speed. Flip & Prince looked out the window at a passing woman. A fine fox. "WOOF! WOOF!" Prince said & made a thrusting motion with her pelvis. "When I see them brown legs out in the street I know I got tuh' get me some."

"Aw man, I like 'em skinny-- so they 'kin get into them positions. Get my cock up against hers & let go! WAHOO!" Flip cried, slapping her thigh.

"Shit, them others is good to me. They 'kin get it too."

"Fat ones."

"Naw, not fat... big bodied. I like somethin' I 'kin grab a hold of at night."

Prince & Flip went on talking as they rounded the corner to the block where SOULVILLE was located. They saw another woman--these were hookers, the streets crawled with them, nevertheless they were still women, and sisters. "Naw, she's too tall."

"Yeah." Flip sighed. "The younger they get, they're getting taller." The hooker was about 15 years old out making her living.

"The woman with me got to act like a lady. And I don't like 'em too tall because it makes me seem short." Prince said. Sometimes they talked about women like they were accessories. Like a hat or a coat.

They went in the club. Blue shadows gulped them up.

The patrons inside turned their heads--the women's eyes were upon Prince, who draped her coat over the back of a chair, a glass of liquor--a Salty Dog at her lips, with a slice of lemon, and salt around its rim.

By 1pm Xenia rushed in, sided up to Prince. They exchanged a few words, Prince waved goodby to Flip, & they departed, arm linked in arm.

Another reason for her success-- Prince was not just a get-on-top butch. Hope-to-die stud. But let her women do whatever they liked to in bed with her.

Prince & Flip both had dildoes, and used them when the situation called for it. Prince had a thick one, short, made of soft rubber, it was pink flesh colored. Prince or her partner would strap it on & they'd use it on each other.

"You let 'em use it on you man?" Flip had asked once.

"Yeah." Prince replied.

This illustrated her great versatility.

Della didn't like fucking her butch with it that much. But Xenia did.

Xenia liked to play. "I'll never get involved again." She told Prince. She was older, she'd been with a man romantically and he'd hurt her. Her affairs with women hadn't been successful either. "I'm not taking life so seriously from now on. Just out to have a good time and enjoy it."

Prince was an ornament to Xenia. Soon the teenager was living with her. But Prince was serious. She wanted a home. She cooked for Xenia and gave her good loving at night.

Prince gave her new woman the benefit of the doubt, but what she had said proved to be true. Xenia wasn't going to take any lover seriously, not for a long long time. So Prince's head began turning to appraise other women once again.

The butch started young. By age 21 she would be jaded. And have a string of women. She loved them. But did she love them more then her gold watch, her mohair floor-length coat, her ruby ring? That is the question!

Yes--she wanted to. These things, keeping up her appearance meant a security in her life. A gut level security that wasn't as lightweight as it might seem. But emotionally she desired a woman, and strove to give her all. It was these things that made her last long in the houses of women she loved--last far longer in their minds and hearts throughout the future, then only a glamorous cardboard doll would have.

16

A few weeks later in the club she met Antonia. Antonia was handsome, also a stud like Prince, but had a feminine flair. Not hard, with men's suits, rather women's suits, boots, earrings. Antonia asked Prince to dance. At this point in her life, Prince was Ki-Ki. Would flip flop in bed. That is, in the gay vernacular, go both ways, butch or femme.--Top or Bottom. "I want a woman who looks like a lady. And acts like one--dresses nice. I don't care what they do in bed." Prince confided once to Flip.

"Well shit, that's the most important thing to me, what they do in bed. They can have a mans suit on, if they get on their back in bed."

"That's you nigger !" Said Prince.

Antonia worked hard. In an office. Saving her money & trying to get ahead in the game of life. Was a strong black woman, and had studied karate. Lived in a black section of town. Prince walked into her apartment. Smell of after-shave and men's hair pomade lingered in the air. A 2 room place, modern furnishing.

In bed, stripped down to the nude, Antonia had a perfect body. Chocolate brown and smooth. Her hair pressed in curls in a masculine fashion. Their bodies entwined in lovemaking. Experiencing the salty taste of each others sweat. Her body was hard from Karate exercises, oiled, both slender & strong.

Chapter Five.

Prince had a buddy, a dude named Alonzo. He was 35, and rode a motorcycle. Was straight. "He knows where I'm comen' from, that I don't take no man putting their hands on me." The two respected each other and were occasional running buddies. Alonzo wore his hair in a short natural, wore motorcycle boots & leather jackets. He was a technician at an aero-dynamics company in South San Francisco.

Alonzo picked Prince up from work one night when she worked the midnight shift. "How was it?" He asked, speaking of her new lover.

"She's good in bed." Prince replied, flatly.

The two rode under the stars at night past the red lights of slower traffic on the highway. They reached the apartment in a jiffy. Alonzo didn't come up. "Good luck he said. Hope this one lasts longer then Xenia."

"If it's meant to be it will." Said she, the two shook hands and parted in the night.

Pretty soon Prince moved in with Antonia--who was quick to tell her that her name meant "beyond praise." They lived together 3 weeks before the relationship began to sour. Prince moved her clothes in tho, and brought her oils that she used to scent her and her loved ones bodies. And the dildo. Antonia used it on her, but this time it was not reciprocal. Antonia was a stud. She avoided being touched. Seldom allowed herself to be penetrated. Prince liked her because she was an attractive woman who dressed sharp. It wasn't important what they did in bed as long as both were satisfied.

Both were taken in by each others appearance. Maybe this is why the relationship didn't work out. Their hearts were fooled-- so busy with a masquerade. The two studs primped in the mirror together, and got each hair in place. One thing was to prove beneficial. Antonia began teaching her young lover Karate. --The art of self-defense.

Also, Antonia was too cheep. She counted every penny. Actually, she, like most women, and most blacks, received a small salary. Whitie wasn't given' up nothing, and so she was trying to make it the best way she knew how. To get a piece of the rock-- some security.

Prince told Alonzo, "We go out-- it's Dutch. I have to buy my drinks. Shit, when I'm with a lady I bought THEM drinks. I'd spend my last dollar on Della."

An evening some time later, Prince broke into the club wearing a 3 piece black suit, platform shoes-- feminine with straps -- had gold posts in her ears instead of earrings, and a necklace of sharks teeth. Her crowning glory her hair, was fluffy, cut shorter then ever before.

She had to work on her hair to keep it looking like that. Nights up in the mirror with permanents, & relaxers & conditioners. Usually spend a good hour styling and blow drying her hair before she hit the club. Except for the shoes she was masculine to a T. And had a hard attitude. Her buddy Flip came in with her looking nice in white pants, white satin shirt, white shoes, a red plaid tie, tweed jacket, her brown hair combed back behind her ears and a silver ring on her hand that said JESUS LOVES, and a Crucifix around her neck, also silver.

Their eyes got accustom to the dim lights. A song came on that all the dykes & sissies loved. The butch women loved it--because the female singer was crooning to them.-- "DISCO MAN!" The fems thought they were the woman saying; "I GOT A THRILL IN MY GAME, TRY ME BABY, TRY ME!" Now the sissies thought THEY were the woman also, and lip-synced the lyrics with their wide mouths, "TRY ME BABY I'M GONNA MAKE YOU SEE! I GOT GOOD KISSES BABY!" Clapped their big hands, switching their lean hips, poked their rounded bottoms out and shrieked in delight.

Prince surveyed the crowd. Blue lights flashed on and off, her face was in profile; and made a famous statement. "..... Sure is a lot of fine women in here tonight... they is women ain't they?" Cold, but warm in her heart. Crisp bow tie at her neck, and that voice of hers, flat. This stiff-legged Sagittarius.

She was broke and pissed. Flip didn't drink but bought Prince one. "What we gonna do?"

"Get loaded & kick ass."

Fairly soon Flip saw somebody she knew and disappeared up among the booths at the club's second level. Prince had been watching a woman across the room, a vision that delighted her soul. "Jazzy ole' Momma, she sure look good to me...." She walked over with the click of her heels like a soldier. The fine brown fem, 5'7", shapely thighs, small breasts stretching out a cloth dress which covered her body; a smile on her face. Beads dangled on her chest. Selima stood at attention like you salute a sergeant in the army--for she saw Prince strutting her way, and was nervous. Had had her eye on the butch all night; as Prince walked down the line, glass in her hand eyeing all the women, Selima followed her with a gaze and managed to catch her eye.

Xenia felt the absence of her young lover and had started trying to catch up with her, but this was difficult as she worked nights. Selima & Prince began to date. The relationship with Antonia had gone dead.

Prince really knew how to love. Loving is more then just tenderness in bed, for a lot of women it is treating them like a lady out of it. Wineing & dining them, buying them presents. Going out on a limb for her. Being good to her. In the clubs & restaurants she treated Selima like a lady. In bed she loved her allnight long. She helped her women with their hair & their clothes. Selected color combinations with an appraising eye. What would suit the woman's figure. For 2 months Prince & Selima dated. Prince had moved back home to her parents middle classed home in the suburbs. She disliked it, but it would have to do, her money was too funny to get her own apartment & she hated to work, missing quite a few days.

The weekends together were good. Selima cooked chicken-- her own secret recipe. Black eyed peas & cornbread. Her hair was short. It didn't grow long but she did wear her own & not some false wig as so many other women did. Selima wasn't beautiful. And she was quiet. Prince told her from the beginning that it was just going to be a casual thing. Just part-time. And Selima agreed.

But, awhile later, Prince told Alonzo on the phone, "She's starting to get serious, and I don't want it. Before it was cool. We'd see each other once or twice a week yuh know... but now all of a sudden she wants me to move in with her."

20

Prince wanted a woman, but unfortunately Selima wasn't it.

Prince really wanted a fo-real woman in her corner. But getting one-- a pearl out of a string of pearls unsuited to her. Not fake pearls, just the wrong shape or the wrong personality to really groove with her own.

To have so many women to her record-- is it blood stains, or blotches of sin smeared into her life book such as those a sinner confesses? No, in retrospect it was only the product of a search that was to take her thru as many beds as there are months on a calendar.-- Year after year. After year!

Yolanda was not a Christian. Hard headed. Determined. She could be cold hearted in her selfishness--unaware of how she was acting. Heels clicked proudly. Head held high. The Henry family was non-religious. And to fill that void Prince had adopted a form of New Age meditation.

The great part of her time was spent looking nice, working & being with one or the other of her women.

If you ever read Jacqueline Susanne's book about the Jet Set, all it is is high class street shit. And that's all this book is about.

Other women's sensuality turns lesbians on --after so long in these mean streets being the only dykes, it's good to hear about your own sexuality. To be validated by hearing other women talk about it. It's fine to hear women get excited over other women. To read about beautiful women who like other women and what they liked to do in bed. & share a sense of camaraderie. Yes, dykes are hungry for books, films, and sex movies about other dykes.

Chapter Six

Prince quit the PALACE for awhile, turned in her cooks hat and went to work at the B.S. FINE Company with her buddy Flip. The light-skinned bulldagger was earning over $10 an hour at the FINE Company. And Alonzo, Prince's Big Brother, or so she called

21

him affectionately, was earning $8 an hour at the aerodynamics company. Finances was an ever pressing problem for the young woman. Her father was earning excellent money as a Mortician and supporting the family with ease. Prince hungered for security of her own. It was a problem that ate away at her lean soul more then anything. More and more. "Man," Flip told her leaning back in the chair, "I'm SUPPOSE to have something. I'm 28 years old! Alonzo is 35, your father is in his 40's. We're SUPPOSE to have something man! You're only 18 years old for Christ sake! When I was your age I didn't have a pot to piss in or a window to throw it out of."

"Mommy's always telling me I'm not doing nothing with my life."

"Well don't listen to her man, shit, I was on welfare until 2 years ago. Shit."

Prince worried alot.

"You're only 18 years old! You've got time man! Now's when you could be trying to figure out what you want to do--like maybe go to college."

3 weeks passed inside the musty office. Rows of tables; florescent lights beamed down at the workers. A clock, cruel, begrudging each second, slowly turned around the hours. One night some of the employees of the office went out for a night on the town. It was February. Cool San Francisco winter.

Katherine, an older white woman, and Dotti, another white sister accompanied them, curious to see a particular establishment in which the two butches spent so much of their nighttime leisure, -- having overheard their colorful and oftimes lurid conversations about the place during the lulls at work; so they stopped by SOULVILLE and had a beer. As they'd walked thru the streets to the club, both butches walked behind talking. Prince & Flip were beginning to look like twins. Prince was subtly teaching Flip how to dress--and improvements could be noticed. Both had on blue caps with the brims down low over their eyes. They took the cement in long strides. Prince reached around Flips neck and fingered her Crucifix.

"What's this, to scare off vampires?"

"Yeah, UH HUH." Flip replied in sarcasm. "Sompthin' like that." Turning to look at her thru lowered eyelids. "Naw man, I just wear it to advertise God, for THOSE who don't know." Said she, signifying about Prince, who was more or less an atheist.

"Aw chump, that's shit." Prince growled.

They arrived at SOULVILLE, soon the party was laughing and talking. Midway thru the night a woman joined the table. Jewel was butch. But fem enough in appearance. 2 earrings in her ears. Slacks & a sweater. Mid-20's. Copper colored. She talked awhile, bought Prince a drink. Then asked her to go home with her & Prince said OK.

They all sat in a booth with red vinyl seat covers. Blue lights from the dance floor turned to green & yellow. The two white women were having a high old time, but grew tired around 1am and left. Jewel, Prince & Flip sat at one end of the booth tapping their fingers to the music.

One of the hangers-on at SOULVILLE was a transvestite who lived in a dream world. The name he had given himself was 'El Greco'. The man was loony, but harmless. He claimed to be bisexual and lived in a world of fantasy which was revealed thru his incredible lies--about his estate in Hollywood, his palatial mansion in the Oakland Hills, etc. The fags would have nothing to do with him, nor would the dykes. He went around with a silly grin on his face--and was in drag constantly. Bridal gowns. Halter tops & bikini bottoms. His long brown legs in high heels.--He was 6'5" tall. In addition, El Greco was one of those black people with a Race Complex. He had to be anything but black. One week he claimed to be part Japanese. The next he'd be going around talking pseudo French, and tipping up to you in his size 14 shoes--high heel pumps-- holding the hem of his dress, his wig, ringlets falling to his shoulders and whisper in your ear: "BONJOUR! COMMA TALLEZ VOUS?" El Greco was dark brown complexioned. Negroid features. Lithe hands which were quite expressive, fluttering at his bosom--a bra stuffed with cloth, or fluttering like Japanese butterflies in air. But, unlike many queer people El Greco had a streak of genius & this is what made him so unusual. He didn't just TELL people he was part Japanese, but he'd go enroll in a school and take up Japanese calligraphy or scroll-painting. He'd buy Japanese language books & really delve into it.

This night, wig in ringlets, El Greco rushed over to the table & greeted the 3 lesbians. This dizzy male in a dress always spoke in falsetto, and in his own inimitable way volunteered the following information, (tho nobody had asked): "I've got 5 bitches working for me. I'm a pimp. They bought me a Cadillac for my birthday last Tuesday."

Prince looked at him thru half-closed eyes and said; "They must be pretty good, why don't you bring one in here so we can meet her."

El Greco's hands fluttered at his face; "I'm on my way home right now, but I'll be back! I have to go! I called a taxi & here it is!" His mouth flapped loosely in his lies.

"What happened to your Cadillac?" Sniggered Prince.

"I let one of my bitches use it." Replied El Greco smoothly, a silly grin on his face.

"Oh." Said Prince.

El Greco picked up the hem of her skirt and twirled around showing her shaved legs. "I'll see you girls later, if you want any Cocaine, any Heroin, pills, anything, just see me, I'll be back!"

"OK El Greco."

And she flitted away.

The departure of the 6'5" drag queen with a sash at his waist & a big bow in his wig brought guffaws of laughter from the booth. Flip had taken her hat off her head and was rolling around in stitches, slapping the table top with the palms of her yellow hands. Big HEE-HAWS came out of Prince & Jewels mouths.

24

Sure enough, El Greco came back 45 minutes later. Now he was dressed in short shorts and a halter top. The rest of his dark body was naked except for a pair of delicate little shoes with two straps, on his feet. He held a tiny sequined purse in one huge hand. He'd forgotten about the Cocaine, Heroin and prostitutes. But circulated around the bar.

Blue lights danced, twinkling silver stars in reflection off empty glasses on the table. "I'm goin' home." Flip stated, laconically. Jewel & Prince sat, wrapped up in each others arms.

Chapter Seven

Jewel dwelled in the Projects. A government building for the poor on welfare aid. Jewel was on AFDC*. She had 5 kids, but they were with her mother so she had to turn over most of the money grant to her. Those evil pink projects Devils Rock they call it. Turrets & spires, blocks wide, and 40 stories high. A few tall buildings, and many smaller ones clustered together in a grotesque squash of crime, addiction, barest survival & misery. The whole thing was covered over sickeningly with a coat of pink paint, like bubble gum. You got stuck there & couldn't get out.

There is no life in the Project, it is made of cement. No place for gardens. No humanity. Humans with their hearts cut out, stand around, eyes agog like broken puppets. Children & adults are caught in its blueprints and iron webs of fire escapes and dangerous stairwells. So they drink all day to escape it. The Negro projects. Other third world people lived here also, and a scattered few poor whites.

Soon after Prince called her Big Brother Alonzo. "All Jewel do is keep me locked up here! We ain't been out fo' two days! She won't let me out of here! She's on Speed. She shoots up those drugs and she's awake for days! I figured I'd wait for her to go to sleep to sneak out, but shit, the bitch never sleeps! She nods off in the corner

25

for a few minutes then gets up & it's back to bed. Fucking. She done fucked me raw! Eat, sleep, and fuck all day."

Jewel had company however, a string of nigger dopefiends, and a particular ladyfriend who eyed Prince knowingly. --Not attempting to hide her interest.

Sadie also lived in the projects, a few buildings down. Coffee with cream colored. Buxom. A woman toughened by life. Had had guns & knives pulled on her by gangsters. And that includes the white police.

Prince had stopped going to work and was just lounging around all day, drinking, smoking reefer and popping a few reds*. One day Flip received a call: "What? Yuh got a new one?" Sez she into the phone.

"Just call me Prince Charming." Sez Prince. "Yep girl, gave her the phone number over to Mommy's house, & she called there all day and all night--nearly drove Mommy crazy. Jewel didn't have no phone. No nothing. I finally got out of there. It was a trap."

Anything to get away from Jewel.

It was an easy move for Prince, from one building colored pink inside the Projects scrawled with gangland graffiti, to another also colored pink, scrawled with a different gangs graffiti; carrying her boxes of clothes like an ant zig zagging over the cement, as seen from overhead.

Sadie was telling folks she was part Puerto Rican, but she acted a purity nigger. Prince used the pay phone in the courtyard of the projects to lament to her big brother: "All we do is lay up in the crib and fuck all day. It's worse then Jewel. Ain't got no money to go no where. Sadie stays drunk. Drunk as a skunk. Ain't nevah seen a woman put away so much liquor. She killed a 5th of brandy--- Hennessey-- this morning & she's up there working on another one now, listening to Isaac Hayes."

*--AFDC: Aid For Dependent Children.

-- Reds: A sedative. Narcotic prescription pill often sold illegally.
--GA: General Assistance.

They did it in every form & position 2 human beings can.
"She can't get enough." Prince said, sarcastically. A combination of
circumstances made her stay, however. She wasn't working and
didn't want to go home and face the music her mother was bound to
play-- namingly "Why don't you get a job and make something of
yourself Yolanda!" Also, it was a route of escape. Prince had applied
for welfare herself. Laying up with Sadie was an excuse not to get
out into the world and try. The handsome woman lay there in the bed
all day popping a few reds, drinking a can of beer.

A month passed. Prince was now collecting her GA* checks--
$47 a month. Della heard about it and wasn't speaking to her. "How
can you let yourself fall so far?" The black woman scolded.

Sunday morning Prince was watching Soul Train on TV. The
large 2 room apartment she and her lover Sadie shared was bare. No
furniture but a bed, and TV & a few kitchen chairs. They never went
out but to use the pay phone or to go to the liquor store. On TV
figures were dancing, and Prince was reminded of SOULVILLE.
How she missed the excitement. All the gay people, the bells, the
music. Even missed El Greco, that man in his dresses. --Around these
projects overrun by burly male gangsters who hated gays, he would
not survive. One brown gal--a tiny figurine on the TV screen posed,
flung her head up in air, threw one hand above her head & marched
across the screen like Cleopatra. Prince yelled feebly from the bed,
"GET IT GIRL! GO 'HEAD!"

"What you say Prince?" Sadie shouted from the kitchen. She
was fixing tortillas.

Now the crowd of figurines in the TV was doing one of those
dance steps that just brought an "ALLRIGHT!" To your lips. But
they were make believe people--and 2nd hand life--that just give a
person a headache.

Chapter Eight

27

For several months Prince's pretty self floated thru the projects. Handsome as she wanted to get. She had took her blow dryer, her hair care kit and her fine clothes over to Sadie's, was getting her welfare checks there, & just didn't have the heart to move again so soon. Was trying to make a go of it, --Sadie herself, plus her environment-- but couldn't take much more.

Prince spent the days being ragged down. A bright spot of pink satin pants suit, blue platform shoes, ad 'fro'd hair among the bleak walls of the Projects as she went about her day, making a precious few phone calls that her coins could afford from her meager welfare allotment-- mostly reversing the charges --and going to the store to shop for food.

This sister always looked very sharp & men harassed her when out in public. One evening Prince was pimped-down in bluejeans with hand-stitched trim she'd painstakingly sewed herself; boots, shirt, jacket to match the jeans, and a tie. This butch had a picture in her mind of what she wanted to bes like. Extremely hi-style masculine & feminine. Sadie wore a dress that showed her nice looking legs; bare arms, a pair of sandals, and her hair in a short natural. A post --gold-- in one nostril, and two gold posts in her ears. They were walking across the courtyard of the Projects. Cool air of evening blew. Women stood in doorways taking ragged wash down off the lines, in housecoats and houseslippers having had no reason to get dressed for the day. Children with sullen faces and no enthusiasm played with wagons and hoops that weren't old but weren't new. It was like a reservation-- a place where people are shoved aside, away from the mainstream, and left to rot.

The whole Projects reverberated with clanging up the spine of it's steel structure, from out of the heart of each separated cubical. Voices that drowned their anger in music & drugs.

Down in the courtyard approaching was a gang of men. The two women saw this, felt themselves freeze taunt inside, but kept walking, being strong. Sadie's big brown eyes with yellowish cast to the orb narrowed. Her jaw was set menacingly, she was a big-boned woman.

28

The gang of young men approached, and a young black punk started some shit. "AH MAN, YO' THINK YO' A MAN!" Yelling at Prince. "WEAREN' A GODDAMN TIE! I OUGHT TO JUMP ON 'DAT BITCHES ASS!" Yells the nigger. Then Sadie took a stand.

"JUST TRY IT NIGGER AN' SEE WHAT HAPPENS TO YO' MUTHAFUCKEN' ASS!!" Howled Sadie; she carried a razor in her bosom, and fished for it now. Her eyes were focused in yellow pinpoints at the young man. The rest of the group jived and shrugged it off, continuing to walk. The youth followed them off, still cursing about bitches wearing ties.

Later that week Prince snuck off to meet Della. The pretty black woman had been calling over to her mothers house in the suburbs, and was worried about her. They met in a restaurant. Sadie was away at her mothers seeing about the kids. Prince asked Della to loan her $20 'till welfare day. But, she told her she wasn't going back to live with her. Della looked attractive, her coat, fashionable with an expensive designer label, lay over the back of the chair in the restaurant. It was her lunch break from work. The waiter had taken their orders. Della had rouge on her black cheeks, bringing just a hint of red blush blended into them. Her lipstick, dark red had the wet look, fashionable in that year of 1975. Her eyes full of concern batted from time to time under her mascara. Prince told her about life in the Projects. She mentioned the incident in the courtyard. "Girrrl, Sadie reached down in her bra, she was going for her razor. She keep it hangin' on a ribbon 'round her neck. She was gonna cut that nigger to bits."

"You wear those ties! Men are going to bother you Prince!"

"That wasn't no man, that was a NIGGER."

"Well niggers, men, you know what I MEAN." Said the middle-- class Della. Prince thought secretly, at least Sadie liked her ties. At least low-classed Sadie who stayed drunk all day thought it was the most natural thing on earth for a butch to wear a mans tie-- being a butch was half man from the get-go; or, for people to be what ever they wanted to be. Even Miss El Greco. It was only when

29

people started getting high-falluten' ambitions that they strove to be like everybody else, to blend in and not create any turmoil.

"Everytime they sees a pretty black woman they has to act ugly."

"Well Prince if you come live with me you won't have to go thru that. Castro street is a good neighborhood!"

"I tole' you that was out."

Prince had pride. The memories of those nights she'd laid in bed alone, moon streaking over the empty sheets from the window, knowing Della was out fucking a man had not rested in her gut easily.-- Instead she'd coughed it up in the form of a resolution. That she and Della would never have a marriage together. In a way it wasn't fair. Della was young and still experimenting with her life. But by the time she'd decided what she wanted it was too late. She'd lost that sweetheart of her teenage years for good.

Chapter Ten

"I'd like to have put my foot in his ass." Prince said, speaking to Flip. They were talking about the tie incident. Flip was an older woman, lines around her mouth, grimly she nodded her head. Wore a man's yellow shirt and a tie herself, the same red tie. Bluejeans and a black jacket. Prince couldn't see this however --how well she was learning to style, under Princes own tutelage, because they were at opposite ends of a phone line--her only source of communication way out in the no-woman's land of Devils Rock. "Put a little liquor in her, and she's CRAZY. Sadie is hot tempered. One thing I likes about her.-- She won't let nobody mess with me. I'm HERS. "YOU BETTA NOT PUT YO' HANDS ON M Y WOMAN!" That's what she told him. Huh. "COME ON DEN' MUTHAFUCKA!" And Sadie goes to spitten' on the sidewalk and shit. Haw haw!"

Chapter Eleven

Nobody saw Prince for 3 months. Locked up there in the pink turrets of Devils Rock with Sadie. Once on Mothers Day--that is, the day the welfare checks arrive --the two managed to make it down to SOULVILLE. Prince's hair had changed style again. Even shorter. And thus, more man-like.

While most women try to hide their heads most of the time hair knotted up, or whitefolks with their hair greasy and straight with no glamour, Prince was always showing her head. It always looked good from the hours of work put into it. But, on the occasions she did wear a hat it was a hat that looked good too. Not a hat just to keep her scalp warm, but to STYLE-- like a flag waving in red. Saying' "Hello! It's me!" Among the crowds of drab people who are anonymous.

Tonight she wore a hat of 3 colors, red, pink and yellow that billowed out. A players hat.

The dancefloor was huge. It extended the length of the building, about 1/4 city block long, and mirrors hung on the walls. Strobe lights flashed off and on, making the dancers silhouettes, then two dimensional, alternating in syncopation. It was Saturday night and the place was crowded with all hard working gay black folks, sipping drinks, greeting each other & sharing a bit of their lives here, in the same point in time.

Prince wore a pair of white overalls-- without a spot, and pressed. A red teeshirt and nothing else. Scented bare arms & chest. White gymshoes--platforms-- which elevated her height by 5 inches. She danced cool. Sadie danced with her head in the air, she was proud to have Prince as her lover to show off --and was conscious all eyes were glued to them. Nobody had seen Prince for months. So THIS was her new lady. Sadie wore a dress --because Prince liked her in dresses. High heels, her big boned body, buxom, stretched out the cloth around the breasts & hips. Her copper colored face had a hint of rouge and lipstick-- all Princes work--very artistic. Sadie tended to be gaudy, but Prince, the master cosmetologist had done her work well, with painstaking taste. Sadie had been surprised herself at how good she looked --it made her feel even freer tonight, and they really cut loose on the dancefloor. Sadie held her head high. Her short brown natural was highlighted by two gold earrings. A smile was on her lips. She strutted like a Peacock.

Back in the section where the booths are, in deep shadows of blues a party was entering and seating themselves. 5 women, two of them studs, the other three ladies, in floor length gowns, diamonds, fur pieces, and wigs in ringlets.

Zabrina was a hefty woman. Combination of brazen and wise. Dangerous and docile. She was a Beautician. Her hair was libel to be blond one night and black the next. Overweight, she poured herself into a too tight dress & still managed to look good. Tan brown complexion. Full lips, heavy make up. She worked a few days a week, and went out & partied the rest. And ate, slept & watched TV. Drinking and popping a few pain pills to ease the stress of life. Zabrina was 36 but just admitted to being 32.

Zabrina sat next to her cousin also an ample woman who wore a blond wig, and was all smiles & dimples. On her other side a big stud who wore a mans suit & hat and had a cigarette in a cigarette holder dangling from her lips. Zabrina eyed the dancefloor with thirst, drinking it up into her soul.

Prince was getting more and more depressed laying up in the projects; a dead end, afraid to go outside-- risking life & limb to make a simple phone call in the public courtyard-- & getting no where. Finally, going back to her parents nagging was better then the boredom, the sense of worthlessness that had begun to creep into her mind. She didn't leave Sadie for another woman but moved back home. It happened after one of their numerous battles. A knock-down, drag-out battle --for anything Sadie did was passionate. And Prince had a violent streak in her as well.

Mr. Henry was just getting off his stint of embalming for the morning at GLORIOUS AFTERLIVES MORTUARY, when he received a phonecall from his daughter. "Daddy! Come on over here & pick me up can you? I got my clothes packed. Sadies at her mothers. I gotta get out of here. She's driving me crazy."

Mr. Henry got in his sportscar and zipped out to the outskirts of town. The walls of the pink palace loomed in the distance & he stepped on the gas, knowing he'd almost reached his destination. Wincing at the sorry plight of lowdown Negritude of these evil surroundings--a place his family had well escaped. He helped his daughter carry out boxes of clothes. They drove off at top speed into the sunset.

Chapter Eleven

That evening Sadie appeared in the club alone. Visibly trembling. Her whole body shook. A snifter of brandy in her hand. Trembling like she'd seen a ghost, and throaty sobs issuing from her poor chest. The copper-colored woman sobbed so hard and so deep she couldn't get the words out; and was strangling on them. "Pppppp Prince. W...w...weee had a a a a....an argument." That's all she would say. Sat there in a booth alone until closing time spending her kids welfare money on brandy after brandy.

Chapter Twelve

During this time Prince unwittingly stepped on not a few toes. A sister stud clued her in-- whispered to her behind the back of her hand: "Be careful Prince, I'm just telling you what I've heard, a lot of people don't like you. Their afraid you'll steal their ladies."

"Well that's THEIR problem." Prince said hotly. She raised her proud head another notch, eyes cold staring into the space of dancefloor where bodies wreathed. "If they can't control their women what do they expect? Women come up to ME! I don't do nothin'!"

"I know, I know man. You're OK wit' me, I'm just tellin' you. Some women in here are angry at you. It's just you should know, so you can keep a watch out."

Prince rode under the stars on the back of the motorcycle. Alonzo's brown face focused on the highway in front of them, and listened to the conversation of his passenger who shouted above the

33

rush of the night air. "THEY'RE GONNA FORM A LYNCH MOB AND TRY TO HANG MY ASS." She was yelling.

A few nights later Prince made her appearance in the club for the second time in a long long while. She gallantly opened the door for her lady, and the couple strutted in on hard heels. All eyes turned. Some with shock. The couple got their drinks and marched across the red carpet, and down the stairs to the dance floor. All eyes turned to witness them. The two stood, drinks in their hands. Prince's features were cold as she appraised the scene. Wearing a full length coat, her fingers dripping in rings. Hair styled short in stud fashion. And beside her in a blond wing the woman whose ample bosom rose and fell under a satin gown that cascaded to the floor, was not Sadie, nor Antonia, or Della, but Zabrina.--The latest in a string of female companions.

Only problem was, Zabrina still had a butch, Maurice, who had gone out of town to Los Angeles.

Zabrina was always surrounded by her cronies. Older women in their middle 30's. Her 'rat pack'. Or her gay Mafia. If you messed with Zabrina, you messed with the whole pack. A loyalty that women need to explore on a broader level.

After Prince relaxed, the effect of the alcohol in her guts, she removed her coat. Tonight the master clothes designer had on her pink satin suit. It clung to her body, uninterrupted by bulges-- she'd had given Zabrina her wallet and keys to carry in her purse. Gymshoes gave her a schoolboyish look-- with the exception that these gymshoes had the latest design, a sole 5 inches thick which elevated her height to a full 5'11" so that like a basketball player she bobbed & weaved among the crowd. All eyes secretly watched her. A slow record came on. Zabrina's eyes blinked, a pleasant smile came over her thick lips. She pulled Prince gently by her pink satin lapels into her, their bodies pressed together, thighs locked together in the eternal position of lesbian passion; the masculine leg pushing the folds of Zairians dress to fit itself into a neat groove, and began to grind; pink-satin pelvis moving side to side with short, firm thrusts in rhythm.

34

That night under strobes & lighting effects surrounded by 300 other celebrating gay women and men, Zabrina & Prince pahteeed -- down!

Along the sidelines, black women styling; ladies in strapless evening gowns, studs ragged- down in blazers and pants, or suits. More then a few women lowered themselves to gossip about something that was none of their business. With the paranoia gay women sometimes exhibit towards each other some mentioned that Prince had slept with everybody in the place--as if she was cheap.

But Prince was young. 19 now. And most of her ladies were in the 24 - 36 age bracket. So it was them who should know better!

The two women left early, as they walked out, along the mahogany bar two familiar faces sulked. It was two of Prince's ex-women talking. Xenia and Jewel. "Why was you attracted to Prince?--It's how she dress? The clothes?"

"No, that ain't true." Sez Xenia. "When I met her she wasn't dressed, she had just got off work. All she had on was pants & a shirt."

"Well she be stylen' even with a shirt & pants." Said Jewel grumbling, looking down the barrel of her beer bottle, eyebrows knitted. To either side of the women the long arc of the bar spread out as far as the eye could see, lined with customers.

"Naw, she had just got off the job, had on her work clothes. Plain-- like a uniform."

"Well her HAIR looked good & she had a ring in her nose didn't she? & how about the shoes?"

Xenia mused thinking back to the night, her brown eyes stared into the dimension of things past-- but things yet longed for. "First time I saw her..."

"But it looked GOOD didn't it." Snapped Jewel, interrupting.--Prince was fresh in her memory having pressed the warm young body to her own not too far back in herstory-- and the hurt lingered. The bitterness apparent.

Xenia had accepted their own break-up philosophically. The romance was, to her good memory stored in her treasure house.--One to be pulled out and mused over in the wee small hours of the morning, alone; when her fingers stroked inside her vulva making solitary pleasure. "Her hair looked bad." Xenia replied.

"It did!"

"Under her hat."

"Sure! Under her HAT! See, she had on a hat! She be stylen' in them hats! She do it for affect-- gets all the mileage she can out of 'em!" Jewel retorted vindictively. Striking her beer bottle down on the bar with a great blow.

"I liked her style." The dark skinny woman confessed, taping her fingers on the bar. "And the second time I saw her she WAS fine. She and her sidekick, some butch that looks a lot like she does. They both got men's suits on."

"Take away her SUITS & HATS and FLOORSHIME SHOES & that's taking away her SOUL." Jewel snapped in a husky voice.

"Yes," Xenia testified dreamily, "the third time she had on one of them leather hats & a leather jacket & leather pants.... And... And..." Embarrassed, Xenia confessed; ".... she was wearen' something inside the pants... I can't say it ... up in the crotch... a big bulge."

"Oh my God."

Soon, a Skunk stripe hairdo would become Princes latest fad.

Chapter Twelve

Most blackfolks had partied that Saturday night away.

A knock came on the door Sunday morning-- a groggy Flip climbed out of bed staggered thru two rooms of her home and answered the door. The yellow woman in pajamas, rumpled, hair sticking up on her head looked at the elderly black gentleman and his companion, an attractive black woman. They were holding booklets & a Bible. They didn't say anything, but gazed at her smiling-- rapture in their faces; so Flip took over. "Are you all from the Jehovah's Witnesses?"

"Yes."

"Well I'm a homosexual! I believe in Jesus Christ, and no where in the Scriptures did Jesus Christ EVER say anything about homosexuals in his ministry. I go to a church for homosexuals and don't have anything to do with any religion that don't like me as a lesbian!" Flip shouted. "SO IF YOU MEET ANY HOMOSEXUALS YOU CAN SEND THEM TO US. THANK YOU, GOODBYE." And slammed the door.

She was tired of being put down. Of being told her sexual preference made her unqualified; and that her lifestyle was inferior-- she was mad about it. And Prince was growing to be more like her every day.

The older bulldagger stumbled back thru the living room into the bedroom scratching her head, her mouth was dry, her eyes half closed--for her sleep cycle had been interrupted--the deep one. Climbed back in bed, but, a few moments later the phone rang.--It was her buddy Prince.

They talked about the latest events in Princes love life. "Daddy tells me when you get a nut it burns up 700 calories.-- Enough for a drink. Have a Martini then get a nut. --2 for the price of one, pretty good."

"Huh." Flip yawned. There was a pause. "Gonna move in with Zabrina?"

37

"No girrrl, I've wised up. I'll never make that mistake again--unless I think it's the real thing."

Prince kept her boxes of clothes at her parents. Her mother was bourgeoisie, and clucked like a mother hen: "Prince, you know you're beginning to look more and more like Flip every day! Men's hats! Short hair! Those CLOTHES!" And meanwhile Flip was starting to dress fancier and fancier--in the impeccable style of Prince.

In a year the young butch's hair had gone from long, rather feminine-- down her back in ringlets, to very short, but still it's natural dark brown. This had happened in stages however, like an freight elevator jerks upwards straining between floors with a heavy load. First she'd cut her hair shoulder length. Then another notch upward, then a page-boy length, then closer to the ears--inching in degrees towards studdom. Finally Prince had begun to dye it-- light brown with a blond streak down the center, blown out in an Afro that was fluff-- like the head of a daffodil.

"Yo' looks like a SKUNK with a stripe down the middle of yo' head." Flip told her.

Life was a frenzy. Women from her past appeared on the scene & they dated. There was Linda a woman she'd gone with at age 13 and 14, even before Della. Prince still took Della out to dinner or a movie occasionally. Or a drive-in with Selima in her fathers car. Beginning a new relationship, with Zabrinia, & beginnings and endings overlapped. And Prince, scurrying here & there to live with boxes of her clothes in her hands, with the blowdryer and hair curlers.

One night Prince was waiting for the bus to take her over to Zabrina's, in San Francisco. She was sitting on a cement bench with a crowd of other people, and a young black man was sitting beside her. The A bus was due in a few minutes. Suddenly the young black man turned and asked her in a rough voice; "SAAY BROTHA MAN, WHAT TIME IT IS !" Made uneasy by his harsh attitude which had startled her out of a reverie, Prince snapped:

"THE CLOCKS OVER THERE!" And pointed to a building--The Oakland Tribune tower, with a round dial illuminated in neon 15 stories high.

The nigger stood up; "MUTHAFUCKEN' BITCH! 'AH DIDN'T AX YO' THAT! I AXED YO' WHAT TIME IT WAS!"

"I'm just telling you!" Prince replied.

"YO' A BULLDAGGER, YO' AIN'T NO DUDE! MUTHAFUCKEN' PUSSY EATEN' B I T C H !" He stood over her yelling.

Prince stood up.

"SIT BACK DOWN!" The man ordered.

Prince didn't budge.

"SIT BACK DOWN THERE!" The nigger ordered again.

"Hey, I'm not sitting down with you up there yelling at me!" She said.

"A GODDAMN BULLDAGGER, MUTHAFUCKEN' BITCH, PUSSY SUCKEN' BITCH, AIN'T GOT NO BALLS! SHIEEET!" The nigger yelled.

"SAY MAN, WHAT YOU YELLEN' AT ME FOR!" Prince said angrily.

"SIT BACK DOWN!" Yelled the man.

Prince stayed on her feet, and her hand shot up; she took a karate stance.

"I DON'T WANT TO GO TO JAIL TODAY!"

"I don't want to go either." Prince said.

"YOU'LL GO TO THE MORGUE!" He hollered.

Prince looked at him, he was right up in her face. His eyes glared at her, his jaws were tight. They were about 2 inches apart. Princes hand rose up, she took the Karate stance again.

The man walked away, hollering and stopped about 15 feet away. "MUTHA FUCKEN' B U L L D A G G E R, YO' LOOK LIKE A NIGGER! B I T C H !! PUSSY SUCKEN' BITCH, YOU BETTER GO EAT SOME COCK BITCH!" The man walked over to the phone booth where three young men stood, he knew one of them. Instantly an item passed from one nigger to him--a silver object-- a razor. Prince saw the glint of metal. Her own knife was in her pocket, but she didn't feel like reaching for it. She felt very very tired, and terribly old. But stood there a moment, just looking at this spectacle of ignorance. One of the youths was trying to pacify the nigger--but hot headed there was no understanding in him. Only fear, fear of what this woman might have in store for him--the absolute death and end of his own weak masculinity;-- and fear of the police kept him at bay. Prince sat back down. She looked at the row of brown & black faces who stared ahead of them, not seeing, ears not hearing.

"What did I do!" She yelled, hands open, a look of bewilderment on her face. The statues beside her said nothing. But gazed ahead. 4 men, big ones, but scared to the bottom of the soles of their big feet.

The nigger was still yelling over by the phone booth, and just then the A bus glided up to the stop. And Prince got up and on stiff legs slowly strutted over to it. Cast one glance back at the scene. The group of men was looking in her direction. Prince threw silver coins into the fare box disgusted. Her steps were stern, falling heavily to the floor, walking down the center aisle. Yellow lights from the interior of the bus shone against the raging night outside. The bus pulled from the curb and sailed away.

The butch sistah continued to testify. In front of her was a white girl dressed similarly. Short blond hair like a crew cut, a mans

40

jacket, shirt, pants and gymshoes. "Didja hear that? Callin' me a BULLDAGGER." Prince said.

"No, I didn't hear anything." The white girl said.

She'd been standing at a distance from the crowd; one of the few whites out there, standing apart from them was a measure of protecting herself. She had been smart.

"That boy callin' me names 'n thangs." Prince continued. She was upset, and had to throw some of the weight of the shit that had just gone down off her chest. Across the aisle were 2 black men. Prince stared at them a moment from out of her brown eyes, but she saw they weren't buddies of the nigger, nor did they look like rowdy types. One was a strong looking brother over 250 pounds, but a softness about him, around his facial expression showed he might be gay. Plus one gold earring in his ear. The other man was the passive type. Prince directed her next words to them:

"MAAN, didja see that fool callin' me a BULLDAGGER!"

"To each his own." Said the strong looking man.

He was trying to shut her out.

"I Heard THAT! That's what I believe!" Prince howled anyway,--desperate for a witness. " What did I DO to him, that's what I want to know!"

Begrudgingly, she got an answer.

"You're pretty strong. I guess you scared him." The man said.

"Yeah, well it's ridiculous. It don't make sense, fighting."

In her heart all the people on that bus knew what Prince had done. The black men knew, the white girl also a lesbian, knew. Prince had been too strong in her gay image. It's not what she had done, but what she was. And once the bullying man had challenged her, Prince had been independent. Stood up for her rights. Been real, not bowing, shuffling, kowtowing to the superior physical strength of an angry, but weak male, use to demanding his way like a spoiled child.

The yellow-lit bus sailed down the thoroughfare. One by one the passengers turned to stare out the windows into the bleak night.

Where did the answer lie?

Prince flirted with the idea of going back there with a gun & teaching the nigger a lesson, but soon all thoughts vanished from her head. To see how hated & feared she was as a homosexual was a meat cleaver punch to the midsection--talking all the breath out of her. It was a situation bigger then life, and formulated upon higher levels then just this one simple incident on the streets.

Yellow lights flickered inside the long narrow compartment of the bus as it rolled over a bump in the highway. Besides them on both side was the blue black Bay water; this bridge crossing over to the Emerald city of San Francisco sparkling like a Jewel. Empire. -- Which lay on the other side. Prince's fair face, with it's freckles was shut tight. Her full lips were closed. Brown eyes stared ahead of her, seeing, but not seeing, boring into the back of the white dyke in the seat in front --thoughts drifting a million miles out.

It wasn't brave.--It had just been that Prince was tired. Yes, she was a lover at an early age, but also was tired at an early age.

Tired of men messing over her. Tired of the white man holding her destiny in his hands. In his pre-arranged society. Tired of being fucked around by people and being taken thru changes.

It's true. A lot of butch's would rather be dead then live on their knees. Call it foolish, but it's war.

It's war out there---this conflict waged between the huge straight world and the much smaller gay one.

In the back of her head, Prince made notes, like a Field Marshall studying the battlefield and examining the corpses that lay strewn about, blood running from their wounds. She noted one thing of great interest --how the men had instantaneously come together in a gang to protect the nigger. A larger more violent man who didn't even need protecting and who was the assailant himself! Saving this observation to remember. How, unquestioning, one youth had handed over his razor.

The bus sped along towards the city. Dark night loomed outside.

'Damn, he went and got a razor.' Prince realized; 'He might have cut up my face. Guess I'll have to get me a gun.'

It made her tired. So tired-- to think about having to carry a gun.

The bus sailed on, had hit the last silver arc of the bridge towards San Francisco. Busdriver was a woman; she maneuvered the wheel. It gave the young dyke a small glimmer of hope thru the leadenness of her mood; that it wasn't completely a mans world anymore. That females were doing things and going places. 'I want to be a busdriver.' She thought. 'There's good money in it.'

Prince had won the battle if anyone had. But, like acid, these things ate away at her. --Her lack of a job; abusive people-- both in varieties of black & white, and males and other women as well. And, worse, there seemed to be no union among women to soften the blows, or, to combat the hate.

'Women have to start getting together and doing something for ourselves.'

Maybe one day she'd learn to walk away from a fight-- and carry on the struggle at a more effective level. Of Gay Rights, and political change. Or, maybe this wasn't the point in life at all. The point in life was just to make a stand at each and every confrontation-- no matter how low and stupid it might seem.

It's called "making a stand."

The odd thing was that, tho he had started the fight, and he was heavier and much more muscular then the dyke, the man had been afraid. She had made her intention very clear. She was going to fight. No wonder he had gone to get a weapon -- inside he was shaking in his boots and his guts were jelly.

She had stood up to a Wrong Nigger and punked him out.

Prince was strong. But in her heart sometimes was so tired of it all she just wanted to curl up and die--and find peace.

There is no sliding by in a war.-- And expect us to have our rights given to us by the enemy. We must make a stand. The only way is to fight. If it means women get into fights and get whipped-- that's the risk for a righteous cause-- but we can't slink away or bow down any longer, or pretend we're ignorant of the situation or make excuse, nor deny what we are. Or pretend worst of all that a threat doesn't exist. We must have a vision of struggling back & then do it.

Men aren't going to change. They aren't going to give their privileges up voluntarily, you can see that. We have to be prepared to make them change. That means we have to fight and will have to fight for the rest of our lives. Are you ready for that ?

Chapter Thirteen

It would be so much better--the life/death struggle, if she had a decent woman in her corner she could come with at night.

Zabrina's house was the 4th story of an apartment building -- she had the whole flat. Soon the two women had cooked a good meal, Prince working at the sink, grumpily, talking little but to answer Z's conversation. The table was covered with a magnificent cloth and set with porcelain plates and crystal glasses. They ate baked fish, beans, rice, salad, greens & garlic bread with butter toasted in the oven. Kool-Aid completed it.

Prince treated her women with respect. She brought them gifts. Gave them glory. Tonight she was empty-handed. Had no cash, but something even better.

The bedroom was plain, walls beige, modern furniture. A mahogany dresser ran the length of one side, cluttered with perfumes, and cosmetics. Two lamps of rose glass on night stands at either side of the bed. Drapes of green sea patterns at the windows, and a spread to match.

The two females took off their clothes. Prince was drained from the evening proceeding plus the large meal, but Zabrina pulled her into her arms and gazed at her with a solemn expression of faithfulness; the woman began to kiss Prince's neck and stroke the curly hairs over her pubic mound. "Let me go down on you baby." Zabrina whispered. "Let me show you my love."

As the woman knelt by the side of the bed massaging Princes white thighs with her brown hands, the butch felt strength begin to flow back into her.

"Come on Prince, stand up, I know you like to feel like the boss, I know what you like & it's OK, I just want to please you." Zabrina looked at her matter-of-fact. She was an older woman and had experienced many different types of sex & personalities. Prince cracked a wry smile, she stood up, legs apart while the woman knelt on the floor beneath her.

"Come on baby."

Zabrina parted the pubic hair with her fingers, gently spread Princes labia lips, then, as her mouth moved to her hard Pearl clit, her hands slipped around cupping Princes butt and drew her body closer. The butch stood, tenseness in her face, arms dangling at her side. The woman's tongue worked wet & thick against her cock and Prince cold feel skyrockets going off in her head.

Maybe it was dominance. Symbol of power, but it was done with understanding between two women. Maybe it was not pure loving and rolling together on the shore of the seas of time knowing

45

no roles in pure love. This is the world however. Prince needed to feel mastery, and so she stood, an alabaster statue, a God, if you will, with a hard face having no expression but pleasure. Put her hands on both sides of the woman's head, firmly gripped it while thrusting her pelvis into that face, working rapidly towards a climax. Prince wanted to feel dominant, and her woman wanted to give her that feeling.

The bedroom door was closed, they were free. Threats of the outside world were forgotten for a time. We love in the world like fragments broken off the wholeness we once had as infants. The purity of life & love, the joy like God. But tho they played games-- and roles it was honest sex. Tho they were not truly in love, there was an understanding of one another's deep needs as lesbians, & as women.

The two nude bodies, white & bronze lay on top of the cover. Prince used oils on her women. Zabrina rolled over on her stomach, kicking her legs in delight. Prince sat on Zabrina, poured the oil onto her back and began to massage it in with strong hands. Kneaded the plump brown flesh between her fingers. Slowly she worked towards her sides, then, laying down her full length on Zabrina's back slid her hands underneath one, caressing her breasts, each full ripe melon in turn; the other reaching down to her pubic mound. The oil made their flesh slide together. One strong hand felt the woman's breasts while the other fingers simultaneously probed between her pussy lips. The friction of her fingers grew stronger. Zabrina uttered a sigh. On the pillow her face tipped to one side, then her big full Negroid lips parted, moaning, her eyelids fluttered. Her hips thrust slowly against the working fingers. Her cock was hot, and growing hard, the nipples of her breasts were erect. Her thrust grew faster against Princes fingers. Meanwhile Prince had begun a motion of her own, pearl clit pressed against the woman's backside. Riding her bootie! Thrusting against it in short jabs. Imagined she was a horseman riding! "Giddy Up! Giddy Up!" The two women came simultaneously, riding the lusty motions of each others bodies.

Neon lights from the street filtered into the bedroom. The two lay there on the covers relaxing. Their hair was sweaty, pushed back out of their faces. Both had gotten a nut. But the night was young and moments like this too rare. Prince pushed a strong hand thru her hair, her freckled face sincere. Rings were still on her hand which smelled of pussy. Now she removed them from her nose to lay effete, on the sheets. Zabrina lay back on the pillows. Prince spread the woman's legs and sought her vaginal opening with her fingers, and pushed inside. She bent down to Zabrina's crotch and placed her lips against the woman's cock, her tongue sought the pearl clit, began licking it while her fingers continued to move in and out slowly inside the woman's vagina in motions growing faster. Faster! Zabrina began to pump her hips, & grabbed hold of Princes curly hair. "Ouuhhhaaa!" She grunted, thrusting rhythmically. The butch's fingers moved in and out of her vagina rapid-fire, greased by the natural flow of pussy juice, while her mouth sucked stronger on her cock, licking her tongue over it fast and strong. In a moment the woman came, letting out a triumphant yell. "AHHH! WHOOO!"

A clock glowed in its luminous dial on the nightstand. Zabrina had gone out to use the toilet, & returned in a diaphanous nightgown filmy over the round curves of her breasts and hips. The two women hugged, sitting on the side of the bed, then Zabrina slipped partially out of the silver gown and lay back on the bed. Enticing! Prince felt strength rising in her once more. Her sex was hot, a knot in her throat. Now it was time to conquer Zabrina! To ravish her utterly-- to take her like a man! Carefully with the precision fingers of a tailor, she fastened the belt & bands around her waist and strong thighs, in a moment strapping on her instrument of male privilege! Her guts tensed with lust as she bent over her partner. Zabrina surrendered once again, spread her legs, bending them back up to her sides, opening up her pussy wide to accommodate her butch's warm body and receive the fucking of his hot lightning fast rod. She encircled his shoulders with firm warm arms, ready to go for a ride; Prince reached down, grabbed the fat meat of his juicy cock in one fist, and began to run the dickhead over Zabrina's spread labia lips, and lowered himself down upon her so the thick shaft of his penis plunged into her, and they were pressed pubic hair to pubic hair- - filling her thoroughly inside! His butt rose & fell as s/he thrust between the fems legs. Conquering her shamelessly! The base of the dick stimulated his own cock-clit. The heat of his orgasm was approaching, his flat white stomach taunt, the jutting male sex organ rose out of his pubic mound appearing then disappearing inside the woman's vagina. His sex turned to jelly--melting out into a tremendous release.

Prince was Zabrina's sweet thang.

She loved that fat woman all that night, all night long. Again and again the two women drove themselves to orgasm. They went for hours. Caressing also, exhibiting tenderness. Humping and grunting and drawing moans from each others lips. The noises 2 human beings make when they copulate.

Prince loved every part of the femmes body. Sucked her breasts & her cock. They slid against each others bodies. Probed pubic hair with tongues & fingers. Became wet with body fluids; and the smell of sex rose to their nostrils. They took turns riding each other and getting a nut that way thigh locked thigh. And again by humping bare flesh, cock to cock, Zabrina's legs spread wide; mashing open the lips of each others labia so their pearl clits were pressed together ecstatically!!

Chapter Fourteen

"Allright all yo' niggers... and ladies... and semi-mens... Time to play cards." Prince strode boldly into the middle of Zabrina's rat pack that was assembled in the back of the flat at the kitchen table, pulled up a chair and sat down. Some smiled at her words, others didn't.

The room was full of women. Studs, skinny, and hefty, in elegant suits, their hair marcelled, eyed the newcomer. Maurice, Zabrina's lover had returned from doing business in Los Angeles. A buddy had clued her in as to the happenings; how her position as butch of the house was in jeopardy. Now Maurice stood, blue and white striped suit, black hair in contrast to her skin a copper color, her nostrils wide, breathing in the heat of the kitchen. Coat sleeves of an expensive cut brushed across the table as the cards were dealt. Zabrina sat enthroned on a kitchen chair, her hair was done up in a snatchback, a dress with a low neckline, rings of diamonds and gold on each finger. The green walls of the kitchen faded up into dusty recess and smoke from cigarettes trailed there. On the stove pots of food simmered adding a pleasant aroma. Other femmes sat at the table talking & laughing. But underneath their joviality was unfinished business that would have to be taken care of before the night resolved. And, everybody, every one of them had in her hands a card.

Now Zabrina hadn't said anything to Maurice, her 190 pound lover because she was cautious of her new little friend. She'd had whirlwind romances before in her 20 year herstory as a gay woman. Prince hadn't asked to move in yet nor given her a ring nor any sign of commitment. Oh, she'd brought flowers and little gifts and spent a little on dips a & dabs but had pledged no permanency. Zabrina was playing it cool. Because she didn't want to wind up with NO lady. Tho she in secret wanted Prince, Maurice, a bulldagger her own age would be better then nothing.

Her butch was a true bulldike--male almost as if by genetics-- since before birth. Mannish gestures and walk with absolutely no hint of the feminine.

Maurice was a handsome woman. Stood against the wall, one shoulder to it, arms folded across her chest belligerently, staring down at the table. A card was in her hands. She wore a pin striped suit, and her broad shoulders bulged inside of it. Maurice pimped for a living. She had women in Los Angeles. Sweat dripped out of her curly black hair. She looked formidable. Carried a razor in her boot and sometimes a pistol in her waistband. Her glass of gin sat on the table.

The room was hot and stuffy. Some of the women nibbled from plates of food. They were tired & hung over from the night before. The weekend party time.

RING RING!

Flip answered her phone. It was Prince. "Girrrrrrl, I just got out of Zabrina's house. Maurice is back! Her stud! I'm lucky to get out of there alive! Everybody's ex-lover was there. It's a regular little Payton Place! And somebody told Maurice about me and her ears was just a'smoken'. We wuz playen' Dirty Hearts. The first

49

heart fell on Zabrina and she asked her ex-lover B.J.

"Did you like it when you went to bed with Cora?"

"Yes."

Then the next heart fell on Cora, and she asked B.J. "Did you like it when you went to bed with Zabrina?"

At the other end of the phone Flip was amused by the portrait of grown women sitting around seriously with cards in their hands, each heart meaning a disclosure of life or death.

"Then it fell on B.J. Now, Maurice had kept saying, "Zabrina is my woman. Zabrina is MY woman." B.J. asked Zabrina:

"Are you Maurice's woman?"

"......... NO."

And then Maurice reached over and grabbed my arm! But Zabrina & them made her let go.

Now when you play Dirty Hearts you're committed to tell the truth. Serious business, because that's what's agreed 'fore you sit down. So we was for real playen'. Soon the room was hot and heavy. The vibes was so thick, the house was buzzin'. Just a regular little PAYTON PLACE girl. So there it was, the way the cards fell. Zabrina had said it in a cold flat voice. Everybody's eyes got real big fo' a minute, but didn't nobody say nothing.

A card fell on Maurice. "Who are you in love with!" She said to Zabrina.

"You know I'm still in love with Mack." She began, opening the conversation with this very leading statement.

"Why didn't Mack come down here tonight!" Asked another woman, upon whom the next heart had fallen.--The women were getting to the thick of it.

"Because Maurice is down here."

"Why did you and B.J. break up?"

"Because she's still in love with me." Cora said, calmly without even batting one of her long heavy coated eyelashes.

Six couples and a few extras sat in the room. Like cowboys of the wild west--or the Civil War. Under sports coats and dresses were all sorts of knives and razors.--The women had thought they was just playen' Dirty Hearts, but actually they'd come to the show-down.

Prince continued: "We squared off in our chairs. Folks taken up one side, or the opposite. Everybody is breathing hard. A card fell. The air was silent and thick. You could cut that air with the edge of a card.

Cigarette smoke oozed.

"Do you still like B.J.?"

"Yes."

Maurice was right there in the room girl.

"Would you go back to B.J. if she said she wanted you back?"

"Yes."

"Was Mack there?" Came the voice questioning over the phone. (Mack had been Zabrina's old man for years; she was a karate expert too.)

"No."

"I KNEW that. Dirty Hearts or not, ain't nobody be THAT honest."

"You ain't never lied girl." Prince continued.

Chapter Fifteen

So, when Prince broke onto the scene, fresh out of highschool and newly 18, this bad bold sistah had her plenty womens.

The teenager was like somebody held back too long, but raren' to go.

She appraised the gay scene that first time; in a reserved manner. From her cool height of 5'6"--increased to 5'11" by a pair of platform boots with silver studs up the sides.

This Sagittarius.

She plunged into it and soon mastered it.

Prince was hep to black idiom, all the latest slang, but also had much style that she invented. Didn't ever talk about it, but she had cultivated her looks--painstakingly. Black stylen', black rap, black walk, jazz, 'n soul.

On a windy street corner Prince's head would turn at the sight of a gorgeous woman, then she'd go after her. Uttering the words, "Jazzy ole' momma, she sure looks good to me!"

Had her a lot of women at an early age. It began in her pre-teens.

To talk about Prince is, number 1, to talk about the clothes she wore-- plus earrings. 3 on the left side and none on the right. Hats, coats, shoes & women-- women were the other accessories which helped glamorize her own image. The more other women saw Prince with different ladies, the more attention she drew to herself, like a magnet. The women figured she must have something to attract all these ladies and they wanted to find out for themselves what it was. Observing them on the dancefloor, in their minds they could act out a pornographic X-rated movie between the two-- thru imagination-- and wanted to step inside the fantasy themselves.

Prince's real needs for these 'accessories' were far deeper tho, then just a surface pastime. She had a gut level need for security. And to her own personality that wasn't idealism of a freedom fighter, or dreams such as an artist builds-- sand castles in air-- it was material stuff. A nice apartment. Clothes. Jewelry. Cash money. Good food. And a good woman who thrilled her and who would stick by her thru all of her shit.

However, her style which she had cultivated, and the many women who chased after her did have the effect of generating a lot of interest around Prince. She was becoming infamous. A sort of Superstar.

It was Yolanda Henry's nature to dress fastidiously. Had been that way as a child.---Dressed to the eye teeth. Would take pains to find out the correct style for butches to wear--earrings; what side, left or right? Then went out and proceeded to get her ear lobe drilled with 5 different holes in a line on that particular side-- a mutilation of her flesh-- so she could wear 4 gold earposts, and one diamond there, glittering.

"Women like glitter." Sez she.

Prince was earthy & you can say she mastered the material. Women gingerly set foot upon her heavy planet.

This Sagittarius seemed to be perpetually old. Those old timers in the club remembered another woman who was 17, a fine black sister, handsome. She had two ladies who she pimped, who bought her a Cadillac as pretty and black as she was.

Until one of her women set her on fire and she retaliated 6 months later with a pistol and both of them went off to the penitentiary for so long a time as no one could now recall their names....

Prince had the makings of a solid gold pimp, but she wasn't the type to exploit another woman. Her background wasn't from the streets, it wasn't a necessity, to her mind, to have to make use of another persons weakness, or to play their love and loyalty into a million dollars. She really loved women. Prince was a woman herself & knew this and it made her angry when she saw women with bruises on their faces, fresh from a beating by some power mad mate. But, from this high moral standard it was also a matter of reconciling her own selfishness & satyriasis.--That is her love of too many women at the same time without hurting some of them.

Many women had seen her standing at the edge of the crowd, freckled face watching solemnly as dancers wreathed. As if in a deep contemplation. Which wasn't all about gold earposts or platform shoes. Yolanda worried a lot about being gay, about the status of women into which gender she was born. The limitations of her race. A triple threat.

At that point in her late teens she was descending lower--tho the days seemed exciting to an onlooker-- for the one living them they were jaded and rang hollow.

No job, no woman she could depend on, not the support she would have liked from her gay- unfriendly parents; it made for insecurity.

Moved into women's apartments to escape the confinements of her parents home. Had to pack her bags and run back home because the women drove her crazy.

Her Mommy subtly implying it's time to 'grow up and stop this gay business' plus urging her to continue school,--which she absolutely did not want to do. Thinking more along the line of some manual trade for a career. Nag, nag, nag. --Thus having to pack her boxes and bags and move out still again!

Yolanda Ann Henry, YAH!

One thing, Prince was cute. Cute, with hard bones underneath. She looked like a fluffy puppy dog, yet you could tell she was tough....

She sewed many of her own clothes and thus looked great in perfect fits. Vests & trousers accentuated her lean form.

Was a tailor, a hairdresser & a seamstress.

People always knew Yolanda Henry was cut out to be something, but we didn't know what.

We were all struggling with the repressive conditions, the lack of a culture for lesbian women in 1975.

As black women we were further oppressed--the circle's in which we had to move were even smaller, while white sisters had carved niches for themselves out of The Rock with facilities such as taverns, restaurants, coffee houses, baseball games, picnics, motorcycle clubs, magazines, counseling centers.

In the vernacular, 'Picken's wuz slim'.

Now as far as fine black sisters, Prince had them all. -- They all had to have some kind of conversation, tho she didn't require an Alberta Einstein.

An important thing to remember was that Prince was a strong woman. Her strength--this must be emphasized. Like a lot of black women, she would take no shit. But also, being openly gay-- a butch, had a lot to do with it. When escorting women public places some males show a lack of respect. The black male in the street in particular. It is not the color of his skin as much as being from a lower economic group-- in which traditionally in brown, yellow, red, or white races, a woman is less then nothing.

At this point in herstory the gay struggle was increasing its dimensions. It was moving out of a motel and barroom life into a political dawning. To be gay was a line drawn on a battlefield, it was no longer all song and disco dance. It was a struggle perhaps more real then black liberation-- at least it had been going on for much longer, since the dawn of herstory. Gender and sex. And in all of it, inexorably tied up with this homosexual liberation, was the ultimate issue of women's rights. The oldest struggle of them all.

Chapter Sixteen

An engine, going, with more confidence gained every day, she moved down the line. Under her hard facade, her defiant black style-- her street hustling, her mack, was a sometimes good heart. The heart was good yes, but the 'sometimes' was her selfishness, and her blind stubbornness--and refusal to see her own mistakes. It was as if Prince worked so very hard to achieve mastery over her material circumstances--every hair in place, her rap down perfect, her clothes immaculate-- that she couldn't bare to think that SHE could be wrong. And, in course of romantic interests-- courting several women at once, she often was wrong.

One night Prince's buddy Flip came in the club. An attractive woman sat in a booth alone. A shapely figure, luscious brown skin, nattily attired in a ladies 3 piece suit, long wig of Chinese hair imported from Taiwan and dainty high heels with tiny straps to hold them on her feet.

Flip drove the woman home, and parked in front of her apartment, expressed an amorous intention towards her. The woman then revealed that she had a lady already. "It's new to me, I've been in the gay life about 6 months. I love Ida, but it's not working. She's got a woman living with her & they've been together for years & she's not about to give her up. I've tried men, they're no good. Now I'm trying women & even that's a hassle. I mean, what's left?" Her brown face turned to look at Flip across the compartment of the car. Her lips were wet with the wet-gloss lip stick, and rays of neon lit her hair. The woman's eyes flashed, she was impatient and angry at her whole situation. Velvet described Ida to see if Flip knew her. "She drives a green Rolls Royce, she's tall--5'10". No, she's not masculine. Always a lady, pants suits, make-up. But she carries a .22 revolver in her purse. She's a bad bitch."

56

Ida was in a powerful position in the Federal Government. This black woman had carved her way up the Rock from the gutters of ghetto streets. She was driven half-crazy in the process by white men, black men & backbiting women. Ida didn't take no mess.

"I think I know who you mean." Flip pondered.

"You've seen her."

Chapter Seventeen

A few nights later both Flip & Prince were escorting the pretty brown woman into the club SOULVILLE. Velvet held her head a notch extra high in the air. Proud. This was another Sagittarius. Prince had been instantly attracted to her. Red & green party lights flashed, but intrigue went on at the table. Velvet told Prince she was already going with Ida, yet the two looked at each other with stubborn sparks of fire in their eyes. Prince's hair was fluffed out in an Afro, almost blond by now, with that white-blond streak down the middle. Wherever she went inside the club she drew attention to herself, lightly bounding in gymshoed feet. Velvet was 25. Another Sagittarius climbing,-- or trying to-- and falling continually back down into the bottom of the barrel. Prince brought Velvet another drink and slid into the booth to sit on the other side of her. Flips yellow fingers drummed on the table, reflectively. The shapely woman lifted the drink to her lips, "thank you, you guys." She said, because tho Prince had went and got the drink, Flip who was working, had paid for it.

Velvet's brown face was attractive, her expression was almost innocent, but her eyes would flash, she'd snap out of it and stomp her foot. This woman had an arrest record from out of town --40b of the Penal Code, solicitation for prostitution. Had been street seasoned in her younger days. She had too much experience to bare up under life's circumstances passively. Anger was always bubbling right under her surface. Shoulder-length hair in luxurious waves. She was full breasted, full hips, an hourglass figure. Dark mascara made her eyes astral. Tonight the three sat in an alcove listening to music as the

57

clock on the wall reflected the hour with a green luminescence. Between the two butches Velvet commanded the show. Wore a jumpsuit, tan, with short sleeves. Expanse of brown arms with a few dark scars on them--left over from her years hustling. A green scarf around her throat.

The two butches were discussing business.

Velvet had retired--she now worked for herself, doing 'massages' out of her apartment. She had no pimp. Ida gave her money and she supported her son who lived with her parents, & herself. Prince was really interested in the woman. A body chemistry had begun to flow between them. Tonight both studs had agreed to spend $50 apiece to go to bed with her. Prince's full lips widened in a smile, her eyes closed half mast as she uttered a dry laugh at something Velvet was saying. "HAW HAW!" Yelled Flip, closing her eyes and slapping the table. Velvet turned to look at Flip drolly for an instant, then flipped her hair with an impatient toss and turned back to gaze upon Prince. That was the difference between Prince & Flip. Sophistication-- bedroom sexiness of Prince-- and the loud humor of the countrified Flip.

Prince had her $50 bill, crisp, folded inside her boots. Flip had two twenties green and rumpled and several tens folded in the pocket of her trousers.

Prince had borrowed $30 of it from Della.

Music ushered them out, bells, & the last pop of the fingers. Gust of cold air. The trio walked up the San Francisco streets towards the car of the yellow-skinned bulldagger.

A room 20' by 15'. Bedroom behind a closed door. The three gay women sat in the living room. Modern furniture--but impersonal. The type that comes with a rented apartment. Candles flickered romantically. Stereo played soft music. The older butch woman sat on the couch next to Velvet, she felt sexual desire rising in her body, turning to look at the woman she was about to have, drinking in the

58

sight, smelling her perfume, physical need blossomed, a longing inside her chest & loins.

Prince sat on the other sofa, legs crossed masculine, a cap on her head, appraising Velvet with knowing looks. The chocolate brown woman had taken off her jacket & vest and slacks and changed into a summer dress for comfort. Soon she would be nude.

Velvet blinked her eyes with a sarcastic expression on her face, flirting with the butch next to her in a mocking way--for both women knew the game that it was--flirting. Flip appreciated the attention tho, and she knew the sensual delight that would fill her for a few brief moments when their bodies clasped.

Sensuality is like a cup, it is never full but for a little while-- then the hunger returns. It is not the same as spirituality, but is part of our physical make-up, to be able to enjoy it.

The two butches savored each instant in the living room, watching Velvet by the flickering light of the candles. Her shapely figure shifted under the dress; round breasts & thighs. The wig was hot, it made her scalp itch so she'd removed it. Cute Afro, short, curled and conditioned was highlighted by gold drops of earrings. Velvets full lips opened to laugh merrily at a joke. A box of marijuana sat on the coffee table.

Flips thighs were hard, her whole body tensed, her guts in a knot, and her sex hot, red hot so that it dripped damp between her legs--creaming in her pants.

20 minutes passed in roundabout conversation. Prince eyes were veiled. Her voice hard, she caught Velvets glance more then once. The bedroom lay beyond the closed door.

"Whose going to go first?" Prince threw the question out into the middle of the floor. A pause, like copper coins dropping into a bucket.

"YOU TWO!" Cried Velvet scornfully, but with humor.

59

Flip licked her lips in anticipation. It had been 2 months since she'd had a woman. Fantasized the scene of brown arms & legs entangled with her tan ones.

In 1972 the T.J.'s sang about those bad Back Stabbers.

An air of competitiveness charged the room, but Prince was patient. Cold and able to withdraw and stand, coolly watching on from the wings--yet not giving up the battle.

Flip and Velvet disappeared into the bedroom & closed the door. Soon the sound of fucking drifted out.

The bedroom big enough for a double bed & a closet behind sliding doors. Nightstand on which sat a lamp and a pink Princess phone. Wood paneling on the walls. A window facing an alley.

Inside, the masculine little woman had stripped down to her teeshirt which she left on, because of hating her breasts. Velvet had thrown her dress on one side of the bed. Had lit a cigarette which was burning in the ashtray. She informed the butch that she had 45 minutes. Flip hastily went down, licking the woman's pussy and squeezing her round firm titties, while Velvet watched her, stroking her head once in a while. Flip came up and embraced her; Velvet's legs bent up at the knees spread back so the butch could get between them; she pressed her cock on Velvet's & began humping. She came in about ten minutes & then went back down to give Velvet an orgasm thru oral sex. Afterwards, Flip laughed. Velvet stroked her straight whitefolks hair with manicured nails, and they talked awhile. Flip wanted to get another nut and Velvet complied, but this time it was more difficult to come. She asked Velvet to go down on her a little bit.

"I'm not suppose to do that, Ida says not to."

"Shit, you was whoring before you met Ida."

Velvet wasn't stealing money from tricks, she earned it, and so she flecked her tongue down Flips stomach in feathery touches

60

then delved into the mound beneath the curly pubic hair and wetly slid down over her pearl clit, perfunctorily. After a few minutes she looked up. "There, that's all I can do. Are you ready now?"

"I'll try it."

Flip got on top of her again and began humping. It took a while. Velvet removed one hand from the humping tailbone which she had been pushing down between her legs in alternate pressure, and took the cigarette from the ashtray where it had been smoldering, and took a puff. When the butch finished she told her to go put on her clothes in the bathroom.

Flip went home, tired & satisfied.

Prince went in the room, and lay down on the bed next to Velvet, the lines of her suitjacket hard, gold buttons glistening on her cuffs, her legs crossed, and gazed into Velvet's eyes. She laid her crisp $50 bill on the nightstand.

"Whatever you want to do baby."

"PRINCE! It's your money! What do YOU want to do?" Velvet cried in a merry voice, quite amused.

"Gaze at you." Replied Prince in a low tone, watching her from under her fluffy Afro like a big puppy dog. Velvet was delighted.

"Oh come on now PRINCE!"

"How long do I get?"

The woman stared at her a moment, suddenly serious, then replied; "All night."

She wrapped her arms around the butch & pulled her down on top of her. Their tongues sought each others mouth in a long French kiss lasting ten minutes.

Prince gave herself to Velvet in cold strength until they knew each other. At the moment of climax their bodies fused together.

Dawn had lightened the window. A cigarette was smoldering in the trey. The two women lay wrapped in each other arms under the sheet. Velvet reached over to the nightstand, picked the $50 bill between two fingers with red nails and handed it back to Prince. "You can save your $money honey." Velvet said, her head held regally, looking down at the curly lambs head that was nestled on the pillow under her arm. She smiled for an instant, holding the butches eyes with an ice & fire gaze.

"Well.... I don't know what to say, but thanks." Prince coolly took the bill back.

Velvet gave a sarcastic little smile--pleased with herself, then flounced her head, reached behind her to the nightstand again, poked under the straw mat on which the lamp sat and withdrew 2 rumpled twenty dollar bills, green, and a ten. Flip's money, and gave that to Prince. "HERE! It's a present! SURPRISE!" And her mouth broke into a wide smile, her eyes twinkled, she clapped her hands like a little child.

"Well....." Prince began, drolly, "... I'm.... blown away. I've never met a woman quite like you before."

"You never will again either." Said Velvet.

"I believe it." Said Prince.

Chapter Eighteen

2 weeks later a car pulled up in front of SOULVILLE, the butches were inside, hat brims pulled low over their faces. Outside the club the gutter was littered with paper. Sissies stood smoking grass in nearby doorways. Inside the car one butch turned to another & spoke: "Go in and see if Ida's in there."

Flip got out, slammed the door & went into the canopied entrance. Came out a minute later. "Naw, she ain't in there."

"Didja look in the toilet?"

"Hell no, I didn't go way back there!"

"Shit! She might be hiding in the bathroom just waiting to blow my head off!"

"Aw maan!"

No joke. SOULVILLE was loosing it's liquor license because a man had been stabbed to death outside in a drug-related argument. & had more then it's share of knives & guns being pulled on folks.

Prince had seen that Sagittarius Velvet & went after her. Would give anything for her. Prince was head over heels in love.

That fateful night before the affair had begun, Prince had told her solemnly, "I have to have you." Stared into the woman's eyes; "I've never met a woman who turns me on like you do. I have to have you --no matter what the cost. I have to sleep with you, even if it's just for one night. Or for a lifetime."

Ida was high in political power. She threatened to have Prince killed. By a professional hit-man. But the teenager had an important thing in her favor. Her father. Mr. Henry was a successful black business man; his funeral parlor was a hub of black enterprise, very well placed in the black community, thus had access to the public ear, and the media. --And that's one person people don't want to mess with. Even the Mafia thinks twice about messing with people with access to instant news coverage.

A few more weeks passed, in which Prince & Velvet continued their mad affair. Prince had gone back to work at the HAMBURGER PALACE, flipping burgers, white cooks cap on her head. Flip picked her buddy up from work at 3AM. The fair freckled face whispered thru the glass partition; "Go 'round the back & see if you see a 1975 green Rolls Royce, and Ida sitten' in it with her .22."

Flip obligingly went out back, but the lot was empty.

"Hey man! If she's threatened to kill you, you better quit seeing Velvet!"

"I love her. Can't stop seeing her. Tried to, but can't get her out of my mind."

"Well man, Ida was going out with her first."

"Ida's got another woman and Velvet's sitting up there on Polk street all alone with nothing to do."

"Well shit man, Ida has warned you to keep away from her, why don't you cool it, and wait for Velvet to break up with her?"

"Velvet won't break up with Ida, because she still loves her. Ida is the first woman Velvet ever loved."

"Well then what the fuck! If she loves Ida cut her aloose! Find somebody of your own!"

"I can't, I love her and she loves me."

"I thought you said she loves Ida!"

"She do. She love us both."

"GODDAMN!" Yelled Flip shaking her head. "Well, I'm telling you, that's my opinion, and I'm not getting involved in this crap! If it was me I'd cut Velvet aloose until she made up her mind what she was gonna do."

Flip gave her warning to Prince. Several days later hell broke out.

Flip picked Prince up after work at 3AM, and they went to an afterhours club frequented by gay folks & hippies. Prince shot pool and Flip wandered around the joint; bought herself a sandwich and a cup of coffee & asked a few ladies to dance. At 4:30AM Ida arrived;

Velvet was at her side, and an entourage of older women who Ida traveled with. The tall woman wore a ladies pants suit, her shoulder bag with the gun slung over her shoulder and readily accessible. But the party was laughing and talking. Drinks in their hands. Suddenly a frown cracked Ida's face. Her eyes turned to cat's slits. Her fingers froze around her drink-- there across the room she saw Prince, you couldn't miss her with that blond hair with the white streak in it. Venomously Ida threw her glass on the floor where it broke, and went charging across the room. Like a fool Prince instead of slipping away thru the crowd came walking towards Ida. Ida's friends were running after her and managed to jump between them & pull the large woman back. Prince had her fists doubled, her chin up in air glaring at Ida.

"GODDAMN YELLOW BITCH YOU KEEP YOUR HANDS OFF MY WOMAN, YOU HEAR ME BITCH!"

Ida grabbed her purse and walked away, followed by her train of friends. Velvet obediently at her side, but a petulant look on her face, her lower lip stuck out.

During the near-fight Flip had slunk around on the outside of the crowd. She had made her decision a while ago back at the PALACE not to get involved--washed her hands of it then. If Prince was going to be foolish enough to keep dating Velvet on the sly. Flip had warned her! Yet she had a feeling of guilt. Of weakness in her gut. Women did need unity and she hadn't even stood up for her friend.

No blows had been struck. Ida was raging mad and stomped up the stairs to the entrance in her high heeled boots. Ida was nearing 40. She was attractive, but had had a rough life--and that was etched into her psyche tho the scars didn't yet show on her face. She was dragging Velvet along by the arm, & outside in the street Ida finally blew a fuse. Near 6 foot tall & mad as hell, right outside the exit she pulled out her gun and struck Velvet on the side of her head-- knocking her on her ass; her wig flew off revealing her short 1/2 inch natural; and she screamed at the top of her lungs:
"AAAGGGHAHGGGGURUURURANGGH
AAGGGGGGGGGGGGUUURRRR!"

"BE COOL!" One of Ida's cronies advised her. "The police rides by here every few minutes! Dis' a hot spot!"

"THIS BITCH AIN'T THE POLICE'S WOMAN, SHE *MY* WOMAN!" Ida bellowed, and socked Velvet again--knocking the pretty woman back down to the cement.

"HELP! IDA STOP IT! STOP IT! STOP HER SOMEBODY GODDAMN IT!"

Ida didn't have time to mess around. Her jaws poked out, she shoved her gun back in the purse and stormed down the street to her Rolls Royce followed by a trail of partygoers in tuxedoes and evening gowns.

Fuming at the mouth Velvet picked herself up from the cement again and stalked after Ida who waited in the Rolls Royce. It took Velvet fifteen minutes to walk 5 doors down to the car so angry was she, lagging & dragging, pissed, but finally she got into the passenger side, and Ida sped off at top speed, saying nothing.

Now that's what you call being hung up on somebody.

Back inside the club Prince's temper had turned violent. "I'M NOT SPEAKING TO YOU! GET AWAY FROM THIS TABLE!" She yelled, holding the poolcue menacingly.

"You don't own this pooltable Prince." Flip said.

Prince glared at her with frozen hate. But Flip didn't move. Then Prince turned away and continued shooting balls off the table with angry jabs. Finally Flip walked out and went home.

Prince told Alonzo about what had happened & said of her ex-buddy; "She ain't got no nuts. No nuts at all."

After that Flip & Prince didn't speak to each other in the club, but coldly walked by each other, when by chance their paths crossed.

Flip felt hurt. She hadn't got involved because she saw thru the whole thing. It was Princes own selfishness that had gotten her into the mess, it wasn't like she was an innocent bystander who some madwoman had jumped on & threatened. Nor was it a political issue around which women's power was being built. But later another incident at the HAMBURGER PALACE was to prove different.

Chapter Twenty

For a while with her women it was a mess. Calling the police. Having locks changed. Getting evicted by landlords. Having assault & battery charges filed against her.

Her hair was bleach blond Afro now. The streak was gone. She had several women and was continuing to see Velvet, but they couldn't get along. Prince was 20 years old.

Prince had to fight with some of her women. Physically knock some sense into their hard heads. Knock 'em down and drag 'em out of clubs 'n thangs. It was turning into an SM trip with Velvet. "All the bitch does is sit up and grin at me when I hit her." She told Alonzo. Velvet was as stubborn as Prince. There was no compromise between them. No wonder they fought. And Velvet was a survivor of street life-- had had so many fists in her face, been slapped around by pimps, tricks, the white police, plus the black ones as well; & rival women, that you could whip her upside her head and she'd only laugh at you.

"The bitch squared off with me last night. Honest to God. She put her fists up in the air, "COME ON! COME ON! YOU WANT TO FIGHT GODDAMN IT!"

But secretly both women's pride was hurt.

During the following months Velvet still spent time with Ida. And Prince met Alexis, Rita, Tina, Eloyce, Velda and Shu-Shen.

She went thru all of them. Laid the women down in the bed naked, fucking & sucking into the wee small hours of morning.

Bodies drained, make up worn off, hair kinked up from sweat. But she didn't form a good relationship with any of them.

Prince quit her job again & was trying to go to school to be a beautician, but the turmoil in her home life was causing her to miss days, even weeks. Often she didn't have enough carfare to get to class. She lived with a string of women, moved in with Velvet, but then they broke up.

Prince was collecting welfare & going to school, but her financial situation wouldn't allow her to make it alone. She needed a roommate--and all her roommates were lovers. She jumped from hell to the fire to the frying pan; back into hell like a goat, climbing on stiff legs. Finally she had to drop out before getting her Cosmetology license, from lack of money. Her mother wouldn't help her because she didn't believe Prince was serious. This hurt the young woman's feelings.

The affair with Velvet didn't die but just went from hot to cold, went dead, and then renewed itself. Each time was a pain to her heart.

Prince would answer her phone with a statement like; "Girrrrlll...." And launch into details of her most recent account of women-who-do-you-wrong. "Velvet's doing out-calls."

"Do she really give massages?" Asked the voice on the other end of the line, "Or is it sex?"

"Velvet never gave a massage in her life. I don't think she knows how to give one. She's turning tricks. She gets $500 for the night. Rich white men."

Or, "Girrrrlll, my tongue is broke. Can't get it back in my mouth. --The muscles in my tongue is broke, all that licken' I done last night.... I licked that pussy until I couldn't lick no mo'."

She told a buddy: "Velvet wants me to go to bed with her, Eloyce wants me in bed with her. I'm only one person! And you know the funny thing about it? I can't get rid of them. Once I meet a woman she hangs onto me like glue! If I had any sense I'd make 'em all go out and 'ho."

"What's your street name gonna be Prince? All pimps got street names."

"Call me DAWG."

"Low down dirty Dawg?"

"Jest DAWG." Cried Prince in a voice dripping with ice & fire. "I'm gonna get me a big house in Berkeley, 8 or 9 bedrooms. One fo' each of my ladies. If they want to be with me they have to ring a bell. I'll lay up in a big ole' bed."

Prince always said she wanted to be a pimp; "Just to try it out and see what it bes like." And by now she had the qualifications. Plenty of women, charm that wouldn't wear out. She could get any lady she wanted. Black ones, white ones, Mexican ones, Orientals, Filipino's; gay ones, straight ones, and both way ones; they all liked her.

Prince went with Velvet off & on for 2 years. Velvet had a son, age 6. Prince was good about kids, always a gentleman around them. Treated them kind. Firm, but kind. She took little Scott everywhere in his cute little suits, or sweater & pants sets she'd buy him from her welfare check. The two could be seen hand in hand. They went to the zoo, to the beach. Went to the store together to buy him a treat. She and the kids formed bonds together. Prince was like a father to each of the kids whose mother was her lady. But, after they split up the women would not allow her to see then any more.-- Out of revenge. Prince was very bitter about that.

When she & Velvet finally broke up that was the end of Prince & Scott too. And it broke Princes heart--by that time she had grown closer to the child then she was to the woman. But she never showed a tear in her eyes.

Chapter Twenty One

"I'm getting cold girl, I really am. Getting so I feel nuthin'....
Just like machine." Prince said, flatly. Round cheeks, her earnest face
full of freckles. She was about to turn 21.

There she sat with her suitcase Velvet had bought her, full of
outfits--her pink satin suit, her turquoise jump suit, her green vest &
matching trousers, her ensembles, her many pairs of platform shoes; -
-not knowing where to go.

"I don't give my full self to a woman anymore. Just go thru
the motions."

People said she is selfish, she won't give. She doesn't know
how to give. That she has cold eyes, and her hair is bleached white.
And her essence is that of a hustler. But she has known pain. You
can say that she won't change. She's made of ice. Won't melt. Is
riveted by fire. That she uses lies. That she wants to hurt, she is a
sadist. Or that she wants to be hurt--to punish herself. A masochist.
But if you say this, you've only seen one side of her. Have you seen
her glassy eyed on pills and liquor--in suppressed hysteria. Yes, she
is selfish-- out for herself, but that is the only side of her that has
learned how to flourish. Only at the very beginning of her romances,
when there is hope-- those first several nights, you can see something
very innocent. But her lovers crush it, and both of them act a fool--
not knowing what a precious thing is just within their grasp. Rolling
over it like a tank. The world which is so straight and hateful towards
gay women helps to crush it too-- as it crushes in on them, and they
turn to tear each other apart in frustration. "Goodnight baby." Husky
women's voices. Warm. Get a nut with another woman. Be cynical.
Used. Needing. Ego. Terrified. Great. Strong. Waiting for the
dawn.

Chapter Twenty Two

Prince had finally become legal after celebrating her 21st
birthday sitting around doing nothing. Jaded at an early age.

After nearly a year of frozen silence, she and Flip had become friends again.

Flip came over to the latest house-- a kitchenette in Oakland. Large room with windows on one side, a hallway and a kitchen with windows that overlooked trees & greenery. The rent was $100 a month which welfare barely covered. Prince stood at the ironing board in her boots, underpants-- tight white crushing her pubic fur. Mans shirt and a cap on her head; cigarette dangling in her lips. Blithely ironing out her trousers.

The 2 buddies went out riding in Flips car. Roaming the streets & seeing what nigger could get into.-- A Bulldagger that is. First they strolled down Telegraph Avenue in Berkeley, window shopping. "Look at that!" Sez Prince, pointing to a sign as they strolled into a clothing store. "It say "No food or drinking inside." But it don't say no smoking. We can burn the muthafucka down!"

Flip had a girlfriend-- a black sister of the God who shared an apartment with the Preacher of the church. The two butches were riding by so they stopped in a moment, but the girlfriend wasn't home. Now the Preacher's usual callers were folks of the church. It was a sanctuary of the Spirit open to all who seek Christ. Gays as well as straights. (They just pretended to overlook the gay part.) Blacks & whites, a Chinese; some Jewish people had recently joined. Most of her callers were gray old men, or women with problems. Now when Prince strolled thru her door in a blazing satin turquoise blue & silver suit, she brightened up the Preachers day immensely. She was a matronly woman, overweight. Her house was sunny and full of bric a brac. Figurines. Paintings--the type that are mass produced and sold in imitation wood frames. Many artificial plants graced the living room in a jungle of green foliage. The two butches took a seat on the sofa. The Preacher eyed them from the divan. The Crucifix with the replica our Savior, his body twisted from it's crossbeam in agony dangling around her neck like a forgotten ornament. She studied the couple of bulldaggers like a thirsty deer panting for water. A pleasant thrill ran down her spine as she drank in the sight. The Preachers little daughter who she'd adopted in a former marriage before she'd turned gay (and then quit being gay for the Fear

71

Of Divine Retribution) came out and grinned shyly-- promptly fell in love with Prince.

"It's the name, it's the name. PRINCE. Kids like that name."

"Aw shit, nigger, you just have charm or something. EVERYBODY falls for yo' hi--yella ass. I don't know what you got but it's sompthin' else." Flip told her after they'd left.

Later in the day Flip returned to the house alone, to see her girlfriend & the Preacher was talking to a Deacon of the church.

"I seen a fine specimen today! God have mercy! A fine specimen just came by here this mawnin'!"

"I see you callin' on God." Replied the Deacon.

"Have to call on somebody." Exclaimed the Preacher. "Honey! God! That was a FINE specimen. Couldn't even eat my cornflakes. I can't get over that fine nigger."

"She said she couldn't eat her cornflakes, huh. Must've been something." Said the Deacon.

"You bring her over as many times as you want." The Preacher turned to Flip and told her. She turned back to the Deacon and told her; "You wouldn't even of seen nothing else for looken' at her."

"Honey chile you better lay down." The Deacon told the Preacher. "You must got a fever."

Flip sat there amongst the plastic ferns cracking up with laughter.

And then the Deacon went back to reading the Scriptures. Out loud: "Their idols are silver and gold, uh huh! The work of human hands! Uh huh! They have mouths but do not speak! Uh huh! Eyes but do not see. Ummmm Huh! They have ears but do not hear. That's Right! Noses but do not smell! HA! They have hands but do not feel; feets, but do not walk; and they do not make a sound in their throat. Those who make them are like them; so are all who trust in them! OH PEOPLE trust in God! God is our help and our shield! OH PEOPLE, put your trust in God! God is our help and our shield!"

Chapter Twenty Three

Evening. Red lights of the gay club. Prince looked like a pimp, wearing a long coat, floor length, beige color--heavy material, like a beach robe. A true pimps coat that swept the floor. Her hair in a blond Afro & rings glittered on her fingers.

Prince had walked like a king thru the gutters blowing with paper in her boots with silver studs, & now strode down the red-carpet towards the bar. She greeted friends with a smile making dimples in her cheeks like a friendly puppy dog, showing her teeth. Her fair skin stood out in the sea of black & brown. Her manicured hands held a glass of gin.

Inbetween her ages of 21 to 22 there was Velda, Shu-Shen, Candy, Dee Dee, Thelma & Isabel Cortez. Velda was a lady she settled with the longest.

Prince still didn't have a car. She was collecting welfare and didn't know what she was going to do with her life. Worked a few odd jobs from time to time, but the money was immediately spent on bills for phone, rent, presents for her ladies, clothes for their kids, fancy rags for herself. Velda drove her home one night & shyly the timid 24 year old batted her mascaraed eyelashes at Prince as she sat behind the wheel; and made her a proposition.

Velda was single. Sweet 'n brown, voluptuous. Was a hairdresser, so her own hair was impeccably styled. She had meat on her bones & Prince liked something to hold onto at night. She dressed sharp. Had recently abandon men to step into the gay life. This was a decision she'd been tossing & turning over many sleepless nights, for years, and finally had got up nerve enough to follow thru. "She likes nothing but light niggers. You should see her ex-old man." Prince related. Velda ran after Prince at a full trot.

Prince wasn't hung up on Velda at first. Velvet was still in her mind, &, by continuing to see her every month or so & refreshing those old embers, was unable to shake Velvet out of her life. Velda had come up to Prince and told her she loved her. And that she would accept her, even on he conditions that Prince would continue to see Velvet and chippy with her on the side. Like faucets of hot and cold running water into a sink, her love for Velvet was gradually turning lukewarm. Prince told Alonzo:

"I made it close to 2 years with Velvet. I don't think I'll ever love another woman like that. I told Velda that I'm still in love with Velvet, it's just that we can't live together."

The following 3 months was spent torn between Velda & Velvet. Both missing her while the other side of their beds lay cold & empty, and no boots with silver studs sat on the floor, and one of her numerous satin outfits missing from its hanger out fluttering around in the streets somewhere.

Prince was demanding of her women as she was of herself. Life was good with Prince --despite two & three days at a time that her young lover would be lost running the streets-- and subsequently, Velda was gaining weight. Eating from worry. They argued. Prince tried to force Velda to diet. Tho an intelligent woman, occasionally a 'dese', 'dem', or 'dose', would fly out of her mouth and Prince would pop it right back down Velda's throat by correcting her harshly. It was the way she did it, not the point she was trying to make. Prince would fly upside Velda's head for arguing back at her.

"You got to knock some sense into 'em." Prince said. "I told her while she was trippen' off that, fuming at the mouth, 'You lucky to have me at all!'"

Was success spoiling the youngster? She was, unawares, taking out her frustrations of being a lesbian in a hostile world, a black woman, and poor--venting this on the nearest target, without stopping to analyze the cause and it's effect. Despite her increasing rage, Prince was still a devoted lover. "Every time I get some $ I buy her something, off the lay-away. A leather coat, those diamond earrings. Got her a full length coat girl, and she went and exchanged it for a three-quarters length coat. Now that shows you how she is. And the woman won't act right. Talken' smart to me & running up to Reno wit' her mother. Women just don't appreciate a good thing. I guess you got to treat 'em like dirt-- then they'll come crawlen' & begging after you."

It was sad but true. This formula seemed to work, and because of it Prince was beginning to cultivate a vicious style.

Velda's side of the pictures was different however. She was sad. Eyes big and moist, hands busy combing out a wig for some customer. "There's days when Prince don't come home--days at a time. And she won't call. I told her, if you aren't going to come home, at least CALL. Don't have me sitting up there waiting on you and you're not gonna show up. But see she won't call because she's afraid that I'll go out in the street and have myself a good time too. And I will, heck yes I will! Me layen' up here, Miss Anne's got my car, no liquor sto'--nearest liquor sto's 8 blocks away. Shit. Now that's not right! She gets to go out but I've got to stay in!"

Prince was taking advantage of her prowess with women. On the side she had a string of others-- but, in the beginning she had warned Velda what it bes like. Flip had a new woman & the woman had a roommate, Alexis. Alexis was a brown skin sister who worked for the government. 27, with 4 kids. She was in love with another butch, but the butch had another lady on the side. Prince asked Alexis to go to bed with her, but for weeks she kept saying no. Was holding on, waiting for the butch she was in love with to act right. Awhile later Prince told Flip, "I asked Alexis last night did she want to get down."

"What did she say?"

"OK."

And so, Alexis's handsome butch, an older woman, brown, putting on weight from years of good living, still wearing her Postal Inspectors badge, came up the front walk on her way to see her woman. Walked into the room, whereupon the smile on her face changed into shock!

For there was Prince curled up on the lady's bed, a pillow under her head, just a pretty as you please.

Chapter Twenty Four

Shu-Shen was half Japanese and half black. Very attractive, curvy figure, big wide eyes slanted like Almonds. Yellowish-brown skin, and growing from her head a huge Afro of jet-black Oriental hair.

Shu-Shen attended the University. Tonight she clutched Prince's arm possessively. Both were dressed to kill. They stood on the floor of JAN'S PLACE a mostly white lesbian bar. "How do yuh do it?" Flip asked Prince, upon seeing her buddy with still another gorgeous lady.

"My secret love potent." She replied.

"Well let me have one of them girls when it wears off."

"Ok, but ain't none of 'em no good.-- I might as well warn you." Prince sez.

Under the spotlight from the ceiling of the club they stood. Prince wore green pants, vest & green jacket--lapels of green suede. A chain to hold the front of it together over her bare chest. Plaid bow tie, spiffy. A pea green cap on her head from beneath which peeked curls of her blond Afro. Diamond cufflinks & a ring of red ruby glittered on her fingers.

Shu-Shen was a woman's liberationist studying to be a lawyer so she could handle women's cases; and was indoctrinating Prince, who was already interested in women's right due to her many prior confrontations with men in countless negative situations from the streets to harassment on the job, or competition in the workplace. At that point Prince was groping for what she wanted to be in life. It was a disappointment to any social-climbing Sagittarius to see how few opportunities were open for women, for lesbians & for blacks--which men were entitled to move into with ease.--But barriers were coming down.

Prince pranced on the dancefloor with stiff legs, never loosing her cool--with just the hint of being a big friendly puppy dog.

Red & black lights. Sea of women dancing. "Why don't you get you one?" She asked of her buddy, the older dyke.

Flip patted her crotch; "I'm saven' it 'till Sat'day. I got a date."

"Girrrl, dis here pussy don't NEVER wear out." Prince growled back in a deep voice.

2AM. They walked to the door. Prince in iron steps, stiff legged surveying the crowd with cold eyes, Shu-Shen bundled up in a maxi-coat tucked under her Prince's arm; Shu-Shen's slanted eyes closed but for a tiny slit thru which happiness twinkled, her lips rounded into a rosebud as of one expecting excitement. Prince & Flip shook hands goodnight at the entrance of the club; Prince was weary. As one satiated, who has experienced all life has to offer. She commented drolly; "We're going to Alohas restaurant, eat, then go home & get a piece. Go home and set my soul free."

Chapter Twenty Five

Nowadays Prince could be seen zipping around town behind the wheel of Shu-Shen's car. She was getting older. Her physique had filled out some. Tho not any fat, not skinny as she'd been in her teens. Her look had grown completely cold.

Would rise at noon, take a quick shower, have a meal, do her hair, drive Shu-Shen to the University then hit the streets 'till time to pick her up again. In the course of her day she might visit Velda or one of her other women.

Seduction. Conquest after conquest. But that hadn't been the original purpose at all... love. Security, a family. That had been her original expectation.

2 butches whispered behind their hands; "There's PRINCE."

"Yeah. 'Shore looks cute. I hear she go wit' studs AND ladies."

"Well I ain't seen her with nuthin' but ladies-- and they bes' finnnnne."

"What I can't figure it is... it's only a piece of ass. After she run her game down on 'dem, or whatever it is she do, when you gets right down to it, it's just her white ass in the bed."

"Aw, it's how she dress and SHAKE dat ass."

"Man, lots of studs in here can't even get ONE woman, much less a whole string of 'em."

"She a hoo-doo, dat' fo' shore'."

Even Flip started to fall for her. She & Alonzo discussed it one night while sitting in the club waiting for Prince to show up; "She wuz just my buddy yuh dig; another stud right? But then I notice, damn, she's goin' with butches! Antonia was butch, and so was Jewel. I sez to myself, whoops, this buddy of yours might be, just might be a lady! Everybody else was getten' some... Just about then I started getting attracted to her."

The handsome man nodded his head. Sturdy brown fingers toyed with a matchbook on the table. He wore a short Afro and leather jacket. His trim figure neatly packaged in a pair of well-fitting trousers. A few sissys were making it a point to walk by the table-- repeatedly--to see if they could catch his eye.

The bulldagger continued: "THEN I noticed we'd go out, riding in the car or something, and I was beginning to get a thrill out

78

of being with her. Get a charge out of it. & then I began to think it was unhealthy."

Chapter Twenty Six

After her whirlwind of lovers there was a section of time in each day where something was missing.-- A job. But this was coming her way soon. By a fortunate coincidence an associate of her fathers in the black business world had been part of an expose on hiring practices in the Bay Area. How many public utilities did not hire black women. Tho they paid equal taxes, they were not represented. This opened the door to the Federal Government establishing a quota of black women & all women that must be hired by the year 1977. Prince went down and put in her application for busdriver. A position that paid $8 per hour.

Maybe she wasn't going to be a pimp after all.

The ghettoized life of a gay black woman had tried to back her into a corner. It had, as a rough sea attempted to capsize her boat. She had been tossed & turned by the tumbling tide. She had grown to maturity in a culture whose structure hadn't been prescribed by tradition.--The gay demimonde. Finding she was a lesbian in a world where any free woman is an outlaw, had been a severe blow that even she wasn't aware of. Lost. Not sure what hope there was for her--by looking at what was happening in their lives she found little validation. A crummy bar in a slum section of town to party in-- amidst backstabbing butches and ladies who flitted from lover to lover at best, and worst, the dopedealers who plied their trade in the restroom, and vicious robberies and even murder outside under the clubs marquee. No places for gay women to assemble together and get collective support--except taverns. Black societies was many degrees worse off then their white counterparts. A dead end. Hard to get a decent job. Where was there for her to go? Or to do?

Her role models were the pimp Maurice, or the hardened Flip living like a hermit working 12 hours a day and having no joy in life-- trying to earn as much money as she could before her fluke job was terminated. Her hero's were the drug dealing Superfly gay blacks who imitated the black exploitation movies. Of iceberg gangstas in highpowered cars.

It was a challenge, carving a niche for yourself in life with no blueprints. In a way this handicap was being turned into a blessing.

Prince was, underneath it all, just regular. Wanted a mate, a home, kids, & food. A roof over her head. Wasn't a greedy nigger. Not out to burn the world down! --Just set it on fire! She might have looked around her once & declared: "There's nothing happening for a gay woman." But we were going to change all that.

On a personal level, Princes problem was that ladies ate up that image of her. Cold, strong, handsome. A turn-on. And, she wasn't ready to give up her suitcases full of satin images. Nor her beauty parlor hours in the mirror, or, her fast living. & turn into a family butch.

Who would be the other half of her fantasy?

Which woman would remain? After the others strayed--or were put out to pasture?

One by one, like copper coins they fell thru a hole in the bottom of her trouser pocket. Ladies didn't work out; they split.

Prince talked about how she wanted a child--a son. She wanted the woman to have kids for her. Spent a lot of $ money on presents. Shoes for their babies. Stylish kicks that cost as much as adult shoes. And little coats and dresses or ties.

She had a good heart; she had not meant to be a playboy nor conspired to that goal, it's just how it had worked out.

She naturally had the secrets-- plus the good fortune of good looks, that, in vain, all the other would-be-players wished they had!

In the beginning she'd really seemed concerned about people. If she told you she'd meet you at a certain place at a certain time she'd be there. If you needed help she'd try to do what she could--

volunteering her services without being asked. If she saw you needed something she tried to get it for you. But thru the years she was loosing this gift.

This Sagittarius was the same all the time. Not moody. Not hot & cold, but consistent.

One night the blond Afro'd young stud walked into the club. Looked at the crowd assembled there; many studs standing on the sidelines, drinks in their hands, forlorn expressions on their faces, their female bodies dressed in a variety of women's or men's clothing. Nice people, attractive, but alone. Then here and there, the femmes. They wore evening gowns, or pants suits. A few styled in bluejeans and army jackets. Earrings, wigs, make up, perfume. And of the 15 or so femmes there that night, Prince saw that she'd had all of them. Nothing else was new in the club. So she turned around and walked out.

Chapter Twenty Seven

Prince wore her green outfit, satin clung to her hard thighs and stretched across her muscular shoulders. A digital watch on her wrist that glowed in the dark. 4 gold rings on the finger of one hand, and on the other two silver plus her red Ruby ring. 3 earposts of gold in her left ear and a diamond. A friend asked; "How many holes yo' got in yo' ear?"

"Fo'. An' gonna get me another one."

The party lights. They're yellow, blue, and green.

This night was special.

2AM, Prince made her usual comment to a buddy; "Guess I'll go eat, go home & get some, then fall asleep." Gave a short laugh.

"Jus' like a nigger." The buddy responded.

Prince should never use drugs.

81

When the crowd of gay folks assembled a few days later to party-down, the gossip they heard circulating thru the subterranean club was that Prince had tried to commit suicide.

"Dat' pretty bright butch?"

"Yeah, PRINCE. She OD'd on pills.--Red's. She in the hospital & might not make it."

Laying up in the Projects--that no-woman's land-- with some woman she'd met. The next morning the lady noticed Prince was awful quiet, slumped in the bed, naked, her green satin suit neatly placed over the back of a chair. Figuring she'd had a hangover she'd let her lay there almost 5 hours while she did her housework-- glancing over occasionally. But then, getting worried had begun to shake her, and slap her-- but Prince wouldn't wake up. Her skin was cold. Not a sound came out of her. Her body was limp and heavy like a dead person with no life left.

The sister had called the police--this was brave of her, because it might mean trouble. But she was more concerned about the value of human life then to worry about what the police might do to her, for being in possession of drugs in the first place. Also she found phone numbers in the handsome butch's wallet and located her parents. At the hospital they pumped Princes stomach. She was in a coma. Soon her father was at her side.

Prince recovered.

When Prince came to she was in a charity ward bed, gray walls spun dizzily around her.

Velvet visited her the 2nd day when she heard the news. It was during their on again off again relationship--during the offs. & Velvet subsequently heard she'd been laying up in bed with another woman when the event occurred. Velvet snatched the fucking IV out of Princes arm; yells: 'BITCH I HOPE YOU CROAK! IF I CAN'T HAVE YOU NOBODY ELSE WILL!"

They had to call the security guard and put her out of the hospital.

4 days later she was released from the hospital & went home. Rested at her parent's house for the following weeks.

She didn't want to talk about it. "I wasn't trying to kill myself. I just took all them pills.

... I was laying up there, back up in the Projects AGAIN. No job. No woman. I'd took a red a few hours before, then I popped another. Got to thinking about things, looked at this woman next to me--she was asleep; then I took another red. Pretty soon I got to looking around me and said, "Oh, what's the use." And I took 5 or 6 more. I just wanted to pass out, to go to sleep and just not wake up."

After that low point, things started an upswing. Her life began to get better. 1 year passed and life slowly was falling into place--like God moves; slowly, but for real.

Chapter Twenty Eight

Getting down to the meat of the story; Prince was treated by all who saw her as an idol. That was dangerous.

"Everybody likes me yeah, but it's no good." Prince said this herself.

Like Elvis Presley, The King of Rock & Roll, her image radiated a lot of sex. Glamour. Fame. She used it in her own way-- to obtain her desires.

She learned that by keeping parts of her personality a mystery that her ladies wanted more and more. Learned to manipulate them. Like she said, "I'm getting cold." Which meant cold hearted.

Prince was an idol. Had cultivated the clothes, the looks. She'd talked the talk, since youth. --Without realizing where it would all lead.

Now this could be positive or negative--depending on how she used it.

Could exploit women--get her own way, never bother to cultivate people because she was aware there were plenty more knocking outside her bedroom door. Never learn to examine her faults, to change her ways, and instead just got by on looks & style alone.

But also, Prince was a strong woman. And women need to see this for their own lives.

Prince had fallen into a trap inside her satin suits; but her audience needed her, irregardless. Women need some zest in their lives. We need other women who are strong. "Yuh need tuh git some glitter in yo' life." As she herself put it.

Gay women need other gay women to look up to for a change.

Like a diamond within a rock, being chipped away, her personality was emerging. Strong. Fastidious about her appearance--every hair in order. People in order also--dependable friends, basically, to be used.

One thing about Prince, she was always the same person. Didn't get into a mood and act all fonky, mysteriously. But always had a reason--at least a reason apparent to her--for any change in behavior. And a justification for her jealousy, or rage.

She had that bitter sarcasm--constantly. A negative attitude from worrying about $; and the lack of respect given to her as a female, & gay.

Respectful of people's homes & possessions. Prince could be trusted.

Was afraid of being shot out in the street at night, without a car, but didn't let it stop her from going where she had to go, or doing what she had to do.

Always sincere.

But this fanatical thing about not being able to see her faults. Was intelligent enough to see other people's side of the story-- but found it difficult to act on this information, or change herself.

A nice outcome, due to Prince's friendship with Flip, that little bulldagger began to dress good. Gradually she came out of her work clothes in which she'd been hiding and broke out in colorful jackets & ties, satin shirts and trousers with a mean cut. Thus managed to pull a few more women--tho they didn't last.

Things people admired about Prince was her manners, her intelligence, her class.

Prince got a woman she settled on--for a while.

Chapter Twenty Nine

"Better get yo' ass jumpin'." She said to Velda.

Velda called Prince 'Miss Ann.'

The pretty sister was seated at the mirror of the dressing table. Her brown face reflected in it. Their apartment was modern, white walls--the neutral color of a rental unit. Sliding glass windows faced out onto a patio. The closet door was open and clothes lay strewn about on the bed, over chairs. A variety of shoes & knee-high boots scattered on the floor. Velda's hand posed in mid air holding a lipstick. A black lace bra supported her big round titties, and a slip sat snugly over her shapely behind.

One of Prince's buddies was standing in the doorway. Prince was across the hall in the bathroom putting the final touches to her Afro, knees bent, ducking down to see herself in the mirror over the sink, both hands working on her head, lightly touching the Afro' pick to it.

At the dressing table Velda's eyes flashed sparks into the mirror. She complained to Johnny, the butch who leaned against the doorway watching the scene--as she had been for nearly an hour-- "I'll get out of here if Miss Ann lets me! First she says my hair ain't right, I should wear a wig. She don't like my dress. SHE wants to wear my brown boots, so that means I have to wear these old shoes and they don't match what I've got on. Nothing I do is right as far as she's concerned!"

That night Prince & Velda gave the butch a ride home and she was spectator to an unusual scene. Midway thru the evening at the club Velda had begun to call Prince by another name-- El Toro, and was playacting that they had just met. Johnny sat in the back seat, quizzical; an astonished smile on her face as the car hurled down the highway with 'El Toro' at the wheel, cap sitting jauntily atop her blond Afro. Finally Johnny said, "Well Prince, if you're 'El Toro' and Velda here is Conchita, then what kind of car is this?"

"A Volkswagen." Replied El Toro--failing to get the point.

"Oh. I though it was a BROUGHAM CADILLAC-- since we is playing everything else, I thought maybe it was something different too."

"Well, in that case it's a Fleetwood." Replied El Toro.

"Well," said Johnny, "if we can do all this then you got 5 ladies in the back of it--for me."

The car hurtled down the highway then turned off at an exit and drove into the residential area. "Where do you live stranger?" Asked El Toro, as if she didn't know; continuing the act. Conchita smiled.

They dropped Johnny off. She slammed the door, still laughing, while 'El Toro' and 'Conchita' drove off into the red sunrise.

It was Prince's versatility that won women to her bed, as well as her hard masculinity. She explained the games she & her lady

86

played; "You been with somebody so long it gets tiresome. Have to spice up life."

Glitter.

In JAN'S PLACE Velda ran into Flip, Prince's sidekick, and soon the two women were talking about her. "Naw, you can't tell her nuthin'." Velda declared. "She's always right."

The attractive Velda shook her head, her full lips glistened with lipgloss. A brown coat rested softly over her curves, she was sad. "It's allright for her to go out and stay all night, but not for me. She goes out and stays gone 2 days--in MY car."

"We can't make it." Prince told Flip about the situation with Velda.

But a week later Prince was vowing; "When I get some $ money I'll pay half the expenses on an apartment for us."

Velda chased Prince, then Prince chased Velda.

They couldn't let each other go.

Another weekend Prince & Velda were out on the town. Tonight she was a Mexican again and so was Velda. Johnny came over to the table. The club was jumping. El Toro looked up solemnly from under her hatbrim at the dark face under it's big natural; "El Johnny, this is my bottom lady, my main ho'-- Rosita."

"Oh." Sez Johnny, going along with it. "How much she pay you?"

"$200 a night."

Again they drove home, the butch in the back seat doing all she could to help from cracking up in laughter--side splitting HEE HAW'S-- but didn't. Not wanting to spoil the erotic moment the two women had going between them.

"Oh El Johnny, you met my sister last week-- Conchita." Velda said, waving with a high handed gesture--by way of explanation, not wanting to have any confusion.

"Well who are you?" Asked Johnny, her face peering quizzically across the compartment of the car.

"ROSITA!"

"OH....... And they dropped me off at the same place?" Johnny questioned feebly.

"YES!"

When Johnny bumped into Velda at JAN'S PLACE a couple of weeks later she asked; "How's Prince?"

"I ain't seen her!"

"Aw, it bes like that, huh?"

"I hope I never talk to her never again in life!" Velda spat.

Chapter Thirty

The sun was setting, red, on buildings of Downtown. The hustlers lounged in doorways, and poolhalls filled with wino's trying to get off the street.

Prince & Flip walked thru this area, known as the Tenderloin. The club SOULVILLE had been right up the street, but it was closed. Shut down by the police.

A drag queen 6'5" tall, in an evening gown with ruffles, a wig with curls descended to his shoulders flounced by. He saw them and cried: 'COMMENT TALLEZ VOUS! BONJOUR!" The two stopped and entered into his insane conversation for a moment as s/he babbled his lies, but at least it was a familiar face among the old haunts.

The two butches walked into the sunset, rapping. "It's been like a whirlwind. I feel like I'm in a tub of water and somebody pulled out the plug. I had a dream in which Della, Zabrina, Eloyce, Velvet, Shu-Shen and Sadie all stood over me pointing their fingers; not heavenly judgment, but earthly hell you might call it."

What can you say about a character so young? That she had the potential to be anything. That if left to her own devices she would make a way for herself--not the traditional way, but her own way. And a valid one.

To search Prince's soul & find out more about her we must read inside.--Between The Lines.

"I plead guilty. I throw myself on the mercy of the court. I've been no good. But this is the job I been waiting 2 years for. It finally came thru. I'm tired of not having nothing to give a woman. They won't have to pay the rent no mo'!"

Her job as busdriver had materialized. Soon she was earning $350 per week.

Later Flip was in a bar downtown, she saw Maurice. The husky woman wore a pinstriped suit. A man's hat, and a cigarette in a gold cigarette holder dangling form her thick lips. "Whatever happened to PRINCE." Said Maurice, with obvious distaste-- spitting the name out onto the vinyl surface of the bar. Green beer ads blinked above her head.

"I seen her at JAN'S PLACE the other night. She broke in the club with 4 of the prettiest women you've ever seen."

"FO'!"

"Yep. And some butches can't even get ONE."

Like I said in the beginning, this book is low-classed street shit. But it does have a definite purpose. The people in it are not real. Any resemblance to anyone living or dead is purely coincidental.--

For they are puppets to illustrate a play. This is an honest book of how life bes sometimes, not a moralistic message. The purpose of it is to validate the existence of a genre of people seldom written about and, until recently usually written off-- discarded by society like an empty bottle in the gutter.

But they have faith in themselves, and they represented themselves in the nightlife; they danced the dance and walked the walk --and so I speak to them, and my purpose is also to put a conscious in them that just won't be shaken. To tell them we have a right to be alive, & everybody else is wrong about us, and the world must be educated. So no one will say; "I didn't know!" And also, with this establishment of our civil rights comes responsibility. For instance, lying to a woman & whispering sweet nothings into her ear while sleeping with her girlfriend behind her back is wrong, because it leaves a broken heart.

When mistakes are made, often it means people aren't following their hearts. Their inner truth.-- Are confused by desire. Become impatient--to capture all the good times they've never got before all at once. Are fooled by a pretty face. Get tied up in false promises.

Humanbeings are three parts. Physical, mental and spirit.

Prince was searching for something... but we never find what we are looking for in the physical or even the mental plane. We act thru these mediums in order to grasp the spirit! There is overwhelming proof of this. For instance the blueprints of the city. Those steel structures and cement, those buildings called The Projects-- The Pink Palace. Mathematically it is correct. The stones will stand until kingdom come. But what of the youths who wither up and die inside them like a blade of grass turns from green to yellow?

It's been said- if someone slaps you in the face, you can cut off their hand and put them in jail. But when they get out, they haven't changed and the next time they see you--having no hand, they'll kick you instead.

The physical battle is not won. There is always a spark of hatred left in that heart. Circumstances aren't smoothed over like a steamroller on a tar road.-- This type of approach is like a city which tears down its slums with a wrecking crane, and forces the occupants to live in metal & cement blueprints--the problem is not resolved, hearts are pinched shut instead of opened up. The dawn of realization into human eyes makes true change. The meeting of hearts in understanding is the only way.

Only a change in the heart. Not all the buildings & blueprints, nor the silver & gold in this entire world can make a difference like a change within.

For a time so much anger was experienced by gay's out in the world. The angry youth at the bus stop-- himself another victim lost. A human face twisted into ugliness. And stopped there forever. A brain abandon to stupidity. A child, like a nut slipped loose, falling among the machinery of Western Civilization--clanging & screaming as he fell.

These stupid and ugly boys, and all the rude customers at the HAMBURGER PALACE, like most men, were not free emotionally. That's a big thing. The whole thing is your emotions. It's how people live their lives--by that. Thru that. And so they'd become as prisoners banging against the iron bars of their jails with tin cups-- begging for something & not knowing what it was.

And the women, afraid; and the gays, moving in shadow, fearful of disclosure of the light-- forever reacting against the violence of ignorant people against them.

It's heavy. It's sad.

Oh how we bang our tin cups against the bars of our jails!

Let imagination describe the spirit of Prince--it was still in the flesh. And there, it was not a slim youngster prancing about on gymshoes 6" tall, but rather a middleaged King in an expensive mink fur coat, fat from rich living like the ancient bards, portly, developing gout from fatty foods & the best liquors. Heavy steps sounding brass in high heeled boots, dripping with rings & jewelry from talons instead of fingers. But no joy. Cruel. Step, step, stepping on, intent on some purpose--to get something material. Bullying her way thru the gray subway stations of the underground.

Her buddy Flip had an advantage--maturity. 15 years her senior. & Flip had been Born Again. Of Spirit. Of her new faith, discovered in the spiritual realm.

In short, Prince had not yet discovered the love from God. Like an idol she'd stare at you as a snake, frozen in anger. A handsome, stone idol, who offered her opponents, or any who disagreed with her no way out. No hope. Whose ears could not hear your side of the story. Whose eyes saw only herself. And used cunning to suck her lovers into her own selfishness.

That is a portrait of an idol. And we all have had our turn at playing that role--inadvertently, or, like a player who holds a hand full of dirty hearts--for all we can get.

Due to Flip's nagging, Prince finally did set foot inside a particular gay church one day. The two butches sat on folding chairs in the living room of a house and listened to the skinny white Minister deliver the message. Now Flip was no holy do-wop goody-goody, as can well be seen by her bar cruising & ho' hoppings. She was fo' real. She had changed but was still the same. Still swore, still got angry at stupidity tho she was learning to forgive. Her wants & personality were intact--they had not been brainwashed out of her by any hellfire & brimstone scare tactics.

The gay church was a large room 30 feet long filled with metal chairs. Most of the congregation was gays who had been kicked out of their own places of worship for being homosexual. The message was inspired. But it fell on hard ears when it came to Prince. The Minister wore TransVestiments of white and black and the collar of the clergy. Before her was a table, and on it were the elements of bread & grapejuice symbolizing the body and blood of Christ. ALL people were welcome! The Minister was starting to give communion.

She held the bread in her hands. Heads were bowed, and many faces wet with tears.

The Minister broke the bread. "Our God welcomes us to the feast."

Now people had started walking up the center aisle to take the Elements; but lights were still blazing in the place--and it was suppose to be dimmed somewhat, for this part of the service, as it was more relaxed and meditative that way. So the Deacon went and pulled the plug to the lamps. It was the wrong one, and immediately the place went dark and you couldn't see a thing, so, hastily she pushed the plug back in the socket--blazing lights came back on. So she pulls out the plug again, so as to plug in a softer light which was right nearby on the piano, but in the pitch darkness the Deacon couldn't find the cord to it, so, back goes the plug, and the lamps go on blazing once more. And that's when Prince bellows: "WHAT IS THIS? STROBE LIGHTS?"

The yellow bulldagger sitting beside her quivered with laughter in her jacket & trousers. Prince shifted in her chair stiffly, hands folded across her chest, hard heeled boots up on the rungs of the chair in front of her, a belligerent expression on her face. "I'd swear we's back at the club with these goddamn lights flashing off & on."

Chapter Thirty One

Flip may have to drag Prince into heaven by her hair showing it's black roots under her Afro--kicking & screaming; teeth barred, when it's her time to go. To scuff leaves joyfully, their feet along the crystal streets of paradise.

Yes God this morning!

Come on out, it's time to be getting ready to go... leaves turned golden unhinge from branches of the trees. The rational person knows it's time; she goes to get her suitcase.... Autumn leaves.....

93

And it all goes into the suitcase, our lives we shed like so many clothes.

One other element yet must be disclosed about Prince. It was the matter she alluded to in the beginning, about her father, when the two bulldaggers first became friends, but later pulled back no punches on discussing it often and vehemently. The fact that her father had committed incest with her, beginning when she was pre-pubescent. And put her in the position of having to avoid his unsavory advances well into her early teens.

The topic would come up, especially when she'd been drinking liquor. Redfaced. Royally pounding the table, with a white ring bedecked fist, while musing over those unpleasant memories in a brooding mood.

Although Prince had no sisters, she discovered that her father had had molested others. He had pulled this same act on his own siblings when growing up. She had had to fight off his lascivious advances and drunken sexual attacks, from the days when she returned from grammar school-- alone, while her mother was out at work-- into their house where he waited for her in some suggestive position with his trousers open-- enduring this up until the time she packed her boxes and moved out at age 15. In addition, something she often suspected later proved to be true, that he was using the bodies of good looking female corpses down at the mortuary for sexual gratification as they were about to be embalmed and prepared for funerals.

When the scandal broke at the GLORIOUS AFTERLIVES MORTUARY his wife, Princes mother, immediately filed for divorce. She retained the house and several bank accounts, and finally realized what her daughter had spoken to her about so many years back, in 1966;-- "Daddy is showing himself to me." "Daddy keeps doing things to me." ---And other charges which Mrs. Henry had vehemently denied, refusing to believe at that time, ---was true.

Was this a part of Princes homosexuality? Probably not. Society more and more has come to realize some people are born to

94

be gay.   But if this sexual abuse profoundly influenced the mature adult, it may have been that magical ingredient which caused Prince's to manifest her irresistible allure. This uncanny attractive ability -- which she would later enhance of course, and add to thru her own brilliant creations-- by which she bewitched many many people in her day.

Which had proved somehow to be not a good thing.

It was a testimony to the damage done by an adults unnatural sexualization of a dependent child at an early age.

Creating a seductress who can get anybody they want.

Shaping a person unable to trust enough to form lasting bonds with anyone.

For now, the Henry family proceeded on as usual, that scandal would not break for several more years. And, as before, Yolanda and her Mommy were estranged.

Chapter Thirty Two

December 1977. Prince was 22. 4 years had passed.

The last incident was that night in the HAMBURGER PALACE with Velvet & Flip.

The trio stopped in to get a sack full of hamburgers, here, where Prince had once worked. Tile floors stretched out, empty chairs of red, blue, and yellow. Deserted tables. Florescent tubes cast their rays down from the ceiling. The cooks labored behind a glass cage, one scrubbing down the sinks for the end of the night, the other flipping the last meat that sizzled on the grill. Sweat ran down their faces. Thru the glass doors, outside the night was black. Cars made their way past, red taillights. 4AM.

They ordered 4 cheeseburgers, 2 hotdogs with chili, 4 bags of fries, a chocolate malt, 2 large cokes, 3 apple turnovers and 3 cups of coffee. It was a large order, and so the three women sat at a table in the corner to wait. Flip was standing at the jukebox, the hatbrim of the blue cap that she wore low over her face. Punching out jazzy music & feeding coins into the box.

Several nondescript black men had come in separately, each ordered a hamburger and a cup of coffee. Then a nigger in a suit with a red vest strode in, a short man about 5'5" but stocky. He had an ugly expression, and stood in front of the glass cage ordering a hamburger & a coke, which was all he could afford with the few coins in his pocket. Eyed the trio who sat, carrying on a conversation. Velvet was beautiful tonight in a floral dress--down to her ankles. Her face painted, lips in pink, eyes startling framed in blue. At first the nigger had assumed the beautiful woman was with 2 Latin boys, but now his eyes pin pointed, his jaw grew tight, one of them--with a curly blond Afro-- had swung a leg over the chair and come strutting up to the counter; whereupon he saw it was not a man but a woman. A bulldagger. Prince had the proud look in her face she always wore--which was more tension then pride. Grabbed a fistful of napkins from a container on the counter and peered into the glass cage to see how their order was coming along. Just then a big brown hand reached over and yanked her bow tie. It was the nigger. Prince slapped his hand away. "GET YO' HAND OFF ME!"

Her bowtie held on, but was lopsided.

The nigger saw red. Rage exploded inside his tiny brain and cusswords flew out of his ignorance, mouth flapping: "GODDAMN BITCH! DO YO' KNOW WHO YO' TALKIN' TO! I'LL KILL YO'!"

The mans face was twisting like rubber, he stood there screaming like a puppet. Velvet & Flip got up from the table and came over, the man saw them, he took a step back: "AH' GOT A GUN IN HEAH!" He cried pointing to his jacket. "AH'LL TAKE IT OUT 'N KILL YO'! DON'T YO' KNOW WHO YOU TALKIN' TO! BITCH DIS' IS SAN 'SCISCO! WE DON'T LET BITCHES TALK BACK TO A MAN IN SAN 'SCISCO! YO' MUST BE FROM OUT OF TOWN!"

Prince yelled at him: "YOU KEEP YO' HANDS OFF ME!"

The yellow bulldagger moved stealthily, reaching into her pocket, took out her knife, opened it and held it behind her back.

The other two black men who had been standing at the counter immediately took sides--they turned to glare at Prince with ferocity, because they identified themselves with the man in the red vest. To them the 2 bulldaggers & any lady who'd be caught being seen with them--were freaks, plus the bulldaggers looked like they were white.

The stocky black man stuck his hand under his coat-- was he bluffing? But he sensed the support from the other two men. "BITCH DON'T YOU KNOW HOW WE DO BITCHES DOWN HEAH! WE TAKE 'EM OUTSIDE AND E V E R Y B O D Y GET A PIECE OF 'EM!"

Prince was enraged, her hands knotted into white knuckled fists held up in front of her face. Velvet stared at the man with wide eyes, a mixture of anger & horror. The man faced Prince, he wasn't looking at the other two women. A distance of 4 feet separated them all.

Flip's eyes were focused on only one thing, the mans hand inside his jacket. She was psyching herself up--the moment she saw that huge hand withdraw with a gun in it, she was going to plunge the knife into the wide target of his chest.

The other two niggers were shifting on their feet and saying loudly to each other-- "YEAH, KILL THE MUTHAFUCKIN' BITCH!"

"YEAH MAAN, 'DAT'S RIGHT! BITCH LOOKEN' LIKE A MAN! SHIEEEET!" --While glaring at Prince.

The white boys working behind the counter did nothing. Not even call the police.

An instant frozen in time.

Prince was cursing a string of noises like a chant-- part of her meditations-- to give her courage-- her fists doubled.

"WHAT YO' DOIN'!" The nigger yelled.

Flip had a gun, a 38. caliber revolver outside in the trunk of her car, which she knew how to use. Would she have to get it? -- Would she be able to get to it? The vision of spending years behind bars in a gray stone jail for mistakenly killing somebody had often flashed before her eyes, and did so now. Prison was in the back of all who were assembled's minds. And all the men, and Velvet had done time there before.

There we leave them. The picture narrows as if thru a telescope, the brighter lit scene of action becomes smaller & smaller engulfed in the surrounding grayness of oblivion.

This scene which has been played & replayed over & over & over unto the very death--the death of black communities all over the United States, the death of all economically challenged groups who occupy their historical place at the very bottom of human existence thru every country, race, language, and time down thru history since time immemorial.

A foolish scene, full of fury that signifies it is born of past hurts compounded by present trifles. Ego. Heartbreak. Liquor. Drugs. Frustration. Pride. All mixed.

At some point--within seconds-- Flip realized the vain foolishness of standing there within the firestorm of escalating rage, and attempted first to pull Velvet away, then Prince. Velvet began to back towards the exit with Flip, but Prince would not leave, so Velvet returned to her side. Proud as a stone idol Prince held her ground, Fists clenched against the threats of guns and curses ringing in the air and would not turn tail and depart.

Flip knew she had the superior weapon--if it would be needed--and was glad to leave the sack of hamburgers, just to get to her gun or drive away and get out of trouble, as she saw it.

Plots end with a fight, or killing, or just hurt feelings.

It was the last straw with Prince & Flip.

Flip thought it was dangerous and reckless to continue to engage in the verbal assault which would soon spill over into bloodshed, when to turn around and leave was still an option. And of course Prince was furious at Flip for backing down.--As SHE saw it, being a coward.

The two hateful strangers were backing up a man they didn't even know, but Flip wouldn't back up Prince, and Flip and Prince were friends!

On the other hand, all three men had jail records. Flip did not. She had avoided the penitentiary by living a more cautious life.

We can talk of plots, who did what, when and why it happened--we can describe it like the cycle of seasons that goes on and on, unbroken. Locked in place. Unchanging. Fate. And this was the problem. About this time, Flip began to grow mighty weary of the non stop circular bar life-- its interchangeable mates, it's sorry dramas, lies and public brawls.

She was tired of playing the backseat to Princes incessant soap opera existence--which was perilous.

To suggest change-- this is how to break the cycle. This is the transcendental plot.

And Prince would not change.

We must be strong for each other. But was Flip going to keep on fighting on such shaky ground-- with little to gain, and so much to loose?

Chapter Thirty Three

Prince was courageous. A sister. And a warrior.

She'd scalp a nigger soon as look at him, with her tomahawk.

But do not get hung up on the word nigger, or on the gender male. For the enemy has many sizes, shapes, colors & sexes.

Vencermos! We shall Win!

Or, as Prince would say --"GO 'HEAD GIRL!"

Let us learn to respect the spiritual force, and not bow to a political trap.

Prince stood there, a born again woman. She had died from an overdose of life at an early age, and now would live to be an old old bulldagger--like ink runs out of a pen getting fainter, and fainter, and finally fades away.

She stood, legs apart, shoulders square in her pink satin suit. Strong-- upholding her own independence like an atlas.

The light of God shines inside her head. Her face grins, it spread from ear to ear!

STORY NOTES:

This story also appears in STORIES FROM THE DANCE OF LIFE Volume II.

At An Early Age was originally published in a volume dedicated to it alone; A Homosexual Story, September 1977, in Berkeley.

I am impressed by the amount of violence in this tale, both out in the hostile public places of the world, it's streets and gay taverns, and inside the interior landscapes of private households. It is a fact more refined 'dykes' did not like to acknowledge existed, but I have rendered the truth.

Also I try not to depart too much from my original texts when republishing--and have not for most of this Early Years Series, but the ending of Me & Prince (an alternate title for the piece) differs radically from the original. I had to make this change, for the original just dies at the end and launches on, with no more plot nor dialogue nor description and merely turns into a religious rant & philosophical sermonizing by which I, in a previous era, attempted to save the world! And today I find ludicrous.

Also I wanted to reveal a reason or cause for Prince's satyriasis & gigolo lifestyle--implicating Mr. Henry-- and provide an ending to that near-Battle Once Again at the HAMBURGER PALACE. I believe the original text is archived in the Bancroft Library, and at the Library of Congress for any to see these difference for themselves.

Some slang used in this story:

"You ain't never lied." This was, briefly, a common expression in the black lower economic milieu of the mid-1970's.

"Piece of the rock." The Rock meaning the establishment. Security. Permanency. To get some prosperity.

"Cock." Originally used to mean both female as well as male genitalia; black slang before 1960's and used quite commonly by various groups.

"Dutch." From "Dutch Treat": Ancient white slang in use in the 1940's and earlier. To go out on a date with both people paying their own expenses, instead of the traditional man pays for everything.

"Grove." 'Get in your Groove'. 'Groovy,' etc. Hippie slang, 1960's, drug inspired. To be high, mellow, feeling good, and have no problems. Used later by blacks.

"Turn them on." To give somebody drugs to get high, or tell them some information, especially some profound enlightened information's that will open up their minds to a greater state of awareness. Hippie/black slang 1960's.

"Ragged down." Black slang '70's 'Rags'--clothes. To be 'down with that;' 'down'-- as in 'pimped down'. So these are the best, baddest clothes in stellar display of haberdashery which turns all heads appreciatively in the nightclub.

"To Style." 'Stylen''. Black slang. Very well dressed. So well dressed it is used as a verb.

"Grass." To smoke grass, slang for Marijuana, hippie derivation 1960's late used by blacks sometimes.

Miscellaneous:

Soul Train was one of the first black centered TV programs in the 1970's. There had not been many others. Amos & Andy show from the early 50s, 60's; which was taken off the air because it was considered to be degrading; too Uncle Tom. For many years Soul Train was the only consistent black show running.

Drag Queen. Transvestite. Freak. 'Man In A Dress'. In the 1970's the word transgender had not yet come into usage--(that word was coined in the early 1990's.) We had the word Transsexual but it was seldom used for gender variants. Not nearly so much as the cruel words above. I am faithful to the rendition of my early work and have not corrected these mislabels.-- In portraying history as it really was. Less was understood about trans folk 'back in the day.'

Person such as El Greco, and miscellaneous other characters in novels & stories of those long ago times are sadly & ignorantly miss-labeled Drag Queens, or 'Men in a Dress.' They are often assumed to be gay men. 'Crazy fags', etc. Today of course they would be known as sex changes in process, or male to female transsexuals. Transsexuals were known about, but the sight of a 'man' unable to totally pass as female was to us, in the 1970's, simply the sight of something odd. A real 'queer.' The more bizarre they appeared, the greater the scorn. -- Despite the fact that many of us were half-transgendered ourselves! There was less of a definition back then, nor space for any middle ground. Those early trans people were putting together a women's style, voice, behavior and ensemble with no help from the outer world; having to grope thru a labyrinth of near-impossibilities to attempt to seize their real gender. In those early days I was primarily recording lesbian, and gay lifestyles. This trans aspect was an afterthought, for it only existed on the periphery of our nightworld; even tho I was later to become one, an FTM. These slangs, references, & descriptions are part of the internalized transphobia we all shared.

El Greco and those TS who surfaced before trans became popular, were the true pioneers, acting exclusively on their inner souls emergence--- not to be stopped by the laughs and sneers and backbiting of those who saw them!

FINAL NOTES:

After earlier being primed by re-reading this data I was entering, first in My Soul Was Red, it was about the end of The Invisible Nigger & then again at the end of The Talisman that I began to notice these stories have the fire of Christ in them! Quotes such as:

"The most important thing is not the winning of the game, but trying.

That's why living in a dust lot instead of grassy yards of suburbs is not the true measuring stick of the worth of a humanbeing. That is why success in a career vs. failure is not the judgment, even of our true selves. But every second of what we say and do. How we try to shoot our best shot against adversity. And just being us.

Folks.

And, God, Who is gambling on people.

This great testing ground called earth.

God's concern for Her people lost, wandering on the mainstreets of this universe." (The Invisible Nigger.)

Comparing the revised stories to the originals (archived in the Bancroft Library UC Berkeley) the reader will find that now the original 'God' word has been changed to 'The Creator' in quite a few places, because I now wish to indicate a greater universality, a God/Goddess by many Names; so as to encompass those of other faiths, which, chiefly, come to mind as being Wiccan, Islamic, Judaic, Buddhist, Native American. However I don't constantly substitute this-- so as not to be redundant and thus lower the artistic standard!

Red Jordan Arobateau
December 2004
San Francisco
Typing onto disc from the documents
Stories From The Dance of Life, et al.
1976, 1977, 1978
Berkeley, CA